This We Believe…and Now We Must Act

This We Believe...
and Now We Must Act

Thomas O. Erb

Editor

National Middle School Association
Westerville, Ohio

National Middle School Association
4151 Executive Parkway
Suite 300
Westerville, Ohio 43081
Telephone (800) 528-NMSA

Printed in the United States of America
Fourth Printing, February 2003

Sue Swaim, Executive Director
Jeff Ward, Associate Executive Director
Edward Brazee, Editor, Professional Publications
John Lounsbury, Consulting Editor, Professional Publications
Mary Mitchell, Designer and Editorial Assistant
Marcia Meade-Hurst, Senior Publications Representative

Library of Congress Cataloging-in-Publication Data
This we believe--and now we must act/Thomas O. Erb, editor.

    p. cm.

  Includes bibliographical references.

  ISBN 1-56090-167-5

  1. Middle schools--United States. I. Erb, Thomas Owen. II. National Middle School Association. III. This we believe (Columbus, Ohio:1995)

LB1623.T48 2001
373.236--dc21   **2001030153**

Contents

Quotations in screened boxes and photo captions in these chapters are from *This We Believe: Developmentally Responsive Middle Level Schools* (NMSA, 1995).

Authors

by order of appearance in this publication

Thomas O. Erb is Professor of Education at the University of Kansas and Editor of *Middle School Journal.*

C. Kenneth McEwin, a Lounsbury Award winner, is a professor of education at Appalachian State University, Boone, North Carolina.

Thomas S. Dickinson, former editor of *Middle School Journal*, is a professor of education at Indiana State University, Terre Haute.

Sue Swaim, a former middle school teacher and principal, is executive director of the National Middle School Association, Westerville, Ohio.

John Arnold is a professor emeritus at North Carolina State University, Raleigh.

Ross M. Burkhardt, former president of the National Middle School Association and former teacher at Shoreham-Wading River Middle School, is an educational consultant in Las Cruces, New Mexico.

Joyce L. Epstein is the director of the National Network of Partnership-2000 Schools at the Center on School, Family, and Community Partnerships, Johns Hopkins University, Baltimore, Maryland.

Marion J. Payne, a past-president of National Middle School Association, is director of Oak Hill Middle School, Milledgeville, Georgia.

Chris Stevenson is a professor of education at the University of Vermont, Burlington.

Barbara L. Brodhagen is a teacher at Sherman Middle School, Madison, Wisconsin.

Gordon F. Vars, a Lounsbury Award winner, is professor emeritus at Kent State University, Kent, Ohio

Deborah Kasak, a former middle school teacher and counselor, is the executive director of the Association of Illinois Middle Level Schools, Champaign.

Jean Schultz is the Coordinated School Health Professional Development Specialist for National Middle School Association, Westerville, Ohio.

Sherrel Bergmann, a Lounsbury award winner, is a professor emerita at National Louis University and educational consultant in Antioch, Illinois.

Preface:
Mission – Improve Middle Level Education

Since its founding in 1973, National Middle School Association has led the fight to improve the education of young adolescents in North America and overseas. During its first seven years of existence, the fledgling association did much to promote middle grades education. However, just what constituted an effective middle school had not yet been clearly defined. Concerned about this situation, John Swaim, 1980 president of NMSA, appointed a committee charged with the task of consolidating in one concise statement the consensus view of the essential elements of middle school education at that time.

After months of deliberation and many drafts, this six-member committee, coordinated by Professor Alfred Arth, submitted a preliminary paper. In addition to Arth, the committee consisted of Professors William Alexander, Conrad Toepfer, Gordon F. Vars, Mr. Charles Cherry, and Dr. Donald Eichhorn. As he has done for so many NMSA publications, including this volume, John H. Lounsbury refined and edited the text. After Board of Trustees approval, *This We Believe* was published in 1982. That edition of *This We Believe* set forth ten essential elements of a "true" middle school and became an influential standard.

Though NMSA has led the battle to provide for young adolescents the type of education they need, the association has not been without allies over the years. In the mid-80s, the National Association of Secondary School Principals tapped three of the educators responsible for writing *This We Believe* to form the majority on its own Council on Middle Grades Education: Professors Arth, Lounsbury, and Toepfer. In addition, Professor J. Howard Johnston and Mr. George E. Melton joined in writing NASSP's (1985) succinct *An Agenda for Excellence at the Middle Level.* This document outlined twelve dimensions of schooling necessary for excellence at the middle level.

The decade of the 80s also saw the publication of numerous tracts calling for the reform of education in the United States. Prominent among these were John Goodlad's *A Place Called School* (1984), Ernest Boyer's *High School* (1983), Theodore Sizer's *Horaces's Compromise* (1984), and the U.S. Department of Education's *A Nation at Risk* (1983). The focus of these reports, however, was primarily on secondary schools.

> Middle level education is the segment of schooling that encompasses early adolescence. The stage of life between the ages of 10 and 15....
>
> While grade configuration may be a consideration, the nature of the program provided for young adolescents, wherever they are housed, is the crucial factor.

By the late 80s, officials at the Carnegie Corporation in New York turned their attention to the plight of young adolescents in the United States. In 1987 the Carnegie Council on Adolescent Development, which counted among its members representatives from the fields of medicine, academia, public school education, state and national government, and the private sector, appointed its Task Force on Education of Young Adolescents. This sixteen-member group included several educators as well as two prominent politicians – Bill Clinton and Nancy Kassebaum. After two years of studying the developmental needs of young adolescents and the conditions in the schools that were established to educate them, the task force issued its report, *Turning Points: Peparing American Youth for the 21st Century,* in June 1989. Decrying the fact that middle grades schools had been virtually ignored in the discussions of educational reform in the decade of the 80s, the task force found "a volatile mismatch . . . between the organization and curriculum of middle grade schools, and the intellectual, emotional, and interpersonal needs of young adolescents" (p. 8). *Turning Points* set forth eight recommendations for transforming the education of young adolescents. This widely circulated volume was instrumental in putting middle level education on the national agenda.

> The second half of the twentieth century brought unprecedented change to modern life, especially to male and female roles, family structures and traditions, influences of electronic and print media, and the increasingly diverse and multicultural nature of communities.

As we entered the 90s, increased attention continued to be placed on the education of young adolescents, with NMSA remaining at the forefront of this movement. Realizing that a decade had passed since the initial publication of *This We Believe*, NMSA officers decided to reissue this seminal document in 1992 with very minor changes. However, as the knowledge base of middle grades education burgeoned in the 90s, it soon became clear that a more thorough reexamination of the status of middle grades education was needed. So in 1994, Sue Swaim, executive director of NMSA, appointed a committee to take a deep look at middle grades education and revisit the previously issued position paper on middle level schooling. In addition to the executive director, the committee consisted of two members associated with the original 1982 document – John Lounsbury and Gordon Vars – and seven other members: John Arnold, Sherrel Bergmann, Barbara Brodhagen, Ross Burkhardt, Maria Garza-Lubeck, Marion Payne, and Chris Stevenson.

In 1995 the committee issued a completely new NMSA position paper on the education of young adolescents under the expanded title of *This We Believe: Developmentally Responsive Middle Level Schools.* This time NMSA's statement defined six foundational characteristics of these developmentally responsive schools and six major elements or program components that would together create the kind of schools young adolescents need and deserve.

To develop further the important ideas in the position paper and give readers more concrete advice about implementing them, a twelve-part series was initiated in *Middle School Journal* under the title "This We Believe and Now We Must Act." It began in September 1996 with Sue Swaim's "Developing and Implementing a Shared Vision," and culminated in Ross Burkhardt's "Advisory: Advocacy for Every Student" in January 1999.

This volume represents NMSA's attempt to further advance its recommendations and make them even more accessible and meaningful to middle level educators and policy makers around the world. Some authors of the 1995 version of *This We Believe* have been joined by a few others to discuss in greater depth those twelve characteristics that would lead to more effective middle grades schooling. In addition to the writing of these authorities, practicing middle level educators were asked to provide indicators that an observer might see, hear, or feel if a particular characteristic of a developmentally responsive middle level education was, in fact, present in a school.

In preparation during the same period as this publication was the follow-up document to *Turning Points*. Written by Anthony Jackson, who was the lead author of the 1989 report, and Gayle Davis, who had been actively involved in national middle grades reform efforts, *Turning Points 2000: Educating Adolescents in the 21st Century* expands and elaborates on the earlier Carnegie Corporation report. The two documents, *This We Believe ...and Now We Must Act* and *Turning Points 2000* provide thought-provoking guidance for those who are not satisfied with the state of education for young adolescents. Unlike standards documents issued by various groups in the 90s, *Turning Points 2000* and *This We Believe and Now We Must Act* examine the entire school experience of young adolescents. By so doing, these publications, alone among the mass of statements being issued, help educators sort out the conflicting recommendations in order to create a total-school program that is concurrently academically sound and developmentally responsive.

Thomas O. Erb
Lawrence, Kansas

January 2001

1. The Imperative to Act

Thomas O. Erb

*W*ho is looking after the whole? ... Few sources were available that examined or related the several content areas to each other in relation to the whole child. ... I would ask here that others think with me about why so few people seem to be thinking, studying, and writing about the nature of the whole curriculum at any level much less K-12. Is it because it has just grown too big for any one person or team of people to grasp? Are scholars and educators so specialized by training and interests that they do not wish to look beyond their specialty? Is there no demand from any quarter for consideration of the whole curriculum?

Whatever the explanation for the current specialized subjects inquiry and standards-setting arrangements, I am not convinced that the learning experiences of children and youth are best served by this division of labor and the seeming lack of conversation about coherent curriculum models. Neither are the teachers and administrators well served who must negotiate alone among the subject areas' demands. (Gehrke, no date [1996], p. 74)

> The importance of achieving developmentally responsive middle level schools cannot be overemphasized. The nature of the educational programs young adolescents experience during this formative period of life will, in large measure, determine the future for all of us.

At about the same time that Natalie Gehrke put her concerns into print, National Middle School Association (1995) responded with the publication of a new vision of what the middle level schooling of many diverse young adolescents should be like – *This We Believe: Developmentally Responsive Middle Level Schools*. This 1995 position paper significantly updated the earlier versions of this vision (NMSA, 1982, 1992). The most recent *This We Believe* described six general characteristics of developmentally responsive schools for young adolescents and then delineated six elements or program components that needed to be implemented in order to achieve schools that displayed the characteristics of successful middle grades schools.

The entire school – the total learning environment – was envisioned. Indeed, the learning experiences of students are not confined by their exposure to separate subject specialists. Students learn from the total experience of a school. As important as the standards movement has been over the past decade, this movement has really consisted of a series of parallel movements each operating in isolation from the others. The work of the math standards writers was not coordinated with the work of the English standards writers, nor that of the science standards writers, nor the social studies writers, who themselves competed with the separate standards writers in history, civics, and geography. As Gehrke lamented, who was looking at the whole picture of middle grades education – or the whole picture of education at any level for that matter? Fortunately, there are now two sources that provide a comprehensive vision of schooling for the middle level. One is the recently released *Turning Points 2000: Educating Adolescents in the 21st Century* (Jackson & Davis, 2000) which follows up on a decade's research and practice subsequent to the original publication of *Turning Points: Preparing American Youth for the 21st Century* (Carnegie Council on Adolescent Development, 1989). *Turning Points 2000* was an attempt to not only refine the elements of an excellent and equitable education for young adolescents, but also to provide more concrete guidance for educators intent on improving their middle schools. In that same manner, *This We Believe ...and Now We Must Act* makes more practical and accessible the basic concepts identified in the 1995 version of *This We Believe.*

There are remarkable parallels between the design elements in *Turning Points 2000* and the characteristics of developmentally responsive middle level schools (Fig. 1). Though the wording varies, four of the *This We Believe* characteristics overlap four of the *Turning Points* design elements. Whereas *Turning Points* combines curriculum and assessment into one element, *This We Believe* separates these into two components. *Turning Points* emphasizes the overarching need to organize human relationships for learning. *This We Believe* breaks this aspect of schooling into three separate parts: flexible organizational structures (teaming), an adult advocate for every student, and comprehensive guidance and support services. Finally, while *Turning Points* describes the need for schools to be democratically governed, *This We Believe* focuses on three of the important outcomes of such governance: a shared vision, high expectations for all, and a positive school climate.

FIGURE 1

Turning Points 2000 Compared to *This We Believe*

Turning Points Design Elements	*This We Believe* Characteristics
1. Teach a curriculum grounded in standards, relevant to adolescents' concerns, and based on how students learn best; and use a mix of assessment methods.	1. Curriculum that is challenging, integrative, and exploratory. 2. Assessment and evaluation that promote learning.
2. Use instructional methods that prepare all students to achieve high standards.	3. Varied teaching and learning approaches.
3. Organize relationships for learning.	4. Flexible organizational structures. 5. An adult advocate for every student 6. Comprehensive guidance and support services.
4. Govern democratically, involving all school staff members.	7. A shared vision. 8. High expectations for all. 9. Positive school climate.
5. Staff middle grades schools with teachers who are expert at teaching young adolescents, and engage teachers in ongoing professional development.	10. Educators committed to young adolescents.
6. Provide a safe and healthy school environment.	11. Programs and policies that foster health, wellness, and safety.
7. Involve parents and communities in supporting student learning and healthy development.	12. Family and community partnerships.

Figure 1 illustrates the points of agreement about the important elements that are required to ensure success for every student, but it is misleading when displayed as parallel lists. In fact, the design elements outlined in *Turning Points 2000* and the aspects of developmentally responsive middle level schools would best be displayed as webs. Much as the human body consists of several separate systems working together (circulatory, reproductive, muscular, skeletal, nervous, digestive, etc.), these elements constitute a system of interrelated parts that function to support each other to ensure success for every student.

One of the most powerful lessons of the past decade is how important it is to implement multiple elements of middle grades reform and maintain those elements over time in order to see positive outcomes for students. Which of the systems of the human body could you eliminate that would not be debilitating if not fatal? Amputations and organ removals may leave a body living, but they leave a body with diminished capacity. So it is with middle grades reform. Flexible structures and a shared vision are important, but without a challenging curriculum, varied learning approaches, and programs for health and wellness, the middle grades school will function with diminished capacity.

A learning environment is very complex. Even attempting to understand just one element – curriculum – in the *Turning Points 2000/This We Believe* scheme is more complicated that it seems at first look. Curriculum for many is the set of standards or goals for student performance. However, this only describes what might be called the "planned" curriculum. Most of the standards statements issued in the 1990s are limited to this narrow view of curriculum. However, what educational planners and standards writers prescribe as the curriculum is not the same thing as what teachers actually teach. The actually taught, or "enacted," curriculum is influenced by several factors in addition to what curriculum guides and standards call for. Furthermore, the curriculum that teachers enact hardly describes the curriculum that hundreds of students will experience day in and day out in a classroom. If the goal is to ensure success for every student, we must be concerned about this "experienced" curriculum.

The curriculum experienced by the various students in a classroom, is a function of many factors, not all of which are under the control of teachers. Official goals and standards are just a part, and perhaps a rather small part, of the curricular experience of students. Joseph J. Schwab (1973), who believed that the school itself ought to be the center of practical inquiry, has provided us with perhaps the best model for understanding curriculum as experienced by students. In his model, subject matter is only one of four major components of curriculum. Since human beings are social creatures, their learning is a social activity that takes place in a setting involving a lot more than a source of curricular information such as a textbook, video, or web site. In addition to subject matter, Schwab insisted on including the students themselves as elements in curriculum. He also included teachers and, finally, what he called milieu, since learning always takes place in a larger societal context. For example, is there any doubt that learning to achieve science standards in a multi-million-dollar physics lab tied to web resources in Silicon Valley and elsewhere is not the same as it is in a converted gymnasium where there are not enough textbooks to go around, no lab equipment, and no web-based computers in sight? Figure 2 demonstrates the complexity associated with just one of the design elements in *Turning Points 2000* and *This We Believe* – the curriculum.

These four elements, each of which has multiple characteristics, interact to produce a learning environment for young adolescents. Carolyn Evertson, Kristen Weeks, and Catherine Randolph (1996) have expanded on this notion of curriculum to define a learning community as involving an interweaving of social and academic aspects. The social aspects include such things as students understanding how to respect and rely on others, how to listen, how to share, and how to be constructive partners and team members. Academic aspects might include engaging students in problem solving, using multiple sources of information, and using computers effectively.

The complex interplay of social and academic aspects or the interactions of the four

Educators serve their students well when they model inclusive, collaborative, and team-oriented approaches to learning.

FIGURE 2

The Four Elements of Curriculum*

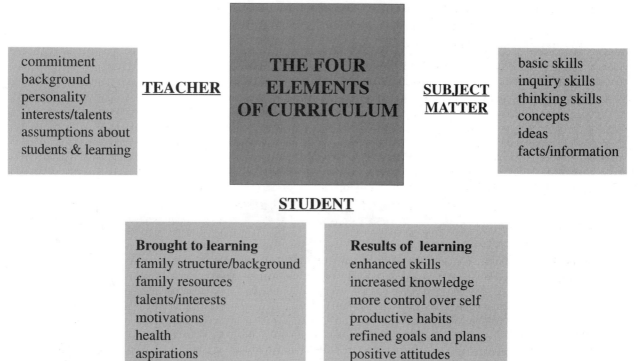

standards and assessments
time of day, season
sound/light/temperature
community expectations
financial support
structures (e.g., teaming)
classroom placement

MILIEU

commitment
background
personality
interests/talents
assumptions about
students & learning

TEACHER

**THE FOUR
ELEMENTS
OF CURRICULUM**

**SUBJECT
MATTER**

basic skills
inquiry skills
thinking skills
concepts
ideas
facts/information

STUDENT

Brought to learning
family structure/background
family resources
talents/interests
motivations
health
aspirations

Results of learning
enhanced skills
increased knowledge
more control over self
productive habits
refined goals and plans
positive attitudes

*Based on Schwab (1973)

elements posited by Schwab offer a caution to those who would reduce schooling to setting standards and assessing them with tests. Though it may be tempting to say that standardized test scores are "the bottom line" in evaluating educational outcomes as profits are in evaluating corporate success, we must not forget that a child is not a "line item." While corporations might be able to fix profit margins by eliminating jobs, we cannot fix test scores by eliminating children! Quite the opposite, we cannot fix schools until every student is successful.

For every student to be successful, each one needs to be supported by a three-legged platform. Beginning in 1994, a distinguished group of people concerned about the education of young adolescents began meeting under the aegis of the National Forum to Accelerate Middle-Grades Reform. With the support of the Carnegie Corporation, the Edna McConnell Clark Foundation, the W.W. Kellogg Foundation, and the Lilly Endowment Inc., this forum has envisioned that high-performing middle grades schools would be (1) academically excellent, (2) developmentally responsive, and (3) socially equitable. The forum's manifesto for middle grades reform has been articulated in the article "Speaking with One Voice" (Lipsitz, Mizell, Jackson, & Austin, 1997). The essence of the ideas contained in *This We Believe* have the support of not only National Middle School Association, but this much broader group of those who are concerned about the fate of our young adolescents.

This We Believe ...and Now We Must Act is designed to help middle level educators better understand the characteristics of developmentally responsive middle level schools and to faithfully implement them. Each of the book's chapters provides a fuller explanation of one of the twelve characteristics. In addition to the chapter text itself, each one contains specific indicators provided by middle level practitioners. These observations identify what one might see, hear, or feel if that characteristic was operative in a school. They help to flesh out the vision embodied in the 1995 version of *This We Believe* and can be used as guides to assist local middle level educators in assessing the current state of their own middle grades reform.

Regardless of where a school may find itself, the explanations and descriptions in *This We Believe ...and Now We Must Act* can help a faculty take the next steps toward a fuller implementation of a true developmentally responsive middle school. We know from the research done on middle grades reform in the past decade (Erb & Stevenson, 1999a, 1999b; Felner, Jackson, Kasak, Mulhall, Brand, & Flowers, 1997; Flowers, Mertens, & Mulhall, 1999, 2000; Stevenson & Erb, 1998) that

Young adolescents form their sense of self in large part from the interactions they have with significant peers and adults.

implementing more elements for longer periods of time does, with certainty, lead to improved student outcomes in all three major goal areas – academic, behavioral, and attitudinal. Yet most schools that are trying to systematically improve have only completed the first part of the journey.

In Turning Points 2000: Educating Adolescents in the 21st Century Jackson and Davis (2000) described the situation this way.

> However, as we have learned over the past ten years, it can be difficult for schools to maintain their momentum for improvement as they get closer to the heart of schooling – classroom practice. Some schools change structures but go no further. In a study of middle schools with excellent reputations, Jeannie Oakes found that, beneath an attractive surface of structural changes, classroom practices and climates had scarcely changed at all (Slavin, 1999, p. 3). Lipsitz, Mizell, Jackson, and Austin (1997, p. 535) recognized middle grades schools' success in making crucial structural changes, but also argued that it is time for schools to stop being merely "poised" for curricular and instructional change and to get on with the job. Without improvements in classroom practice, the goal of ensuring success for every student will remain out of reach. (pp. 28-29)

Jackson and Davis (2000), in the concluding chapter of *Turning Points 2000,* give their call to action and challenge in these words.

This book should also stand as an affirmation of the enormous progress in improving middle grades education that has been made not only in the past decade but also since the "movement" began many years earlier. It is also a statement – not *to* the community of middle grades educators, but *from* that community – that we are not satisfied with the quality of middle grades education today and we know there is a great deal of difficult work ahead. And that we accept and are capable of meeting the challenges we face. (p. 219)

This We Believe ...and Now We Must Act (NMSA, 1995) along with *Turning Points 2000* (Jackson & Davis, 2000) are the only sources currently available that will really help educators and policy makers see the whole picture regarding middle grades school improvement. The standards promulgated by the separate disciplinary associations – useful as they are – and the assessments produced by the several states – politically necessary as they are – provide only a framework for reform. Neither provides specifics on how to construct learning environments that truly lead to student growth and development. *This We Believe ...and Now We Must Act* is such a source. Keep in mind as you review each chapter, while it is important to understand the dimensions of each element of reform, it is also important to realize that these elements are not just additive; they are interactive. The more of these elements that can be implemented over long periods of time the more likely you will be able to demonstrate to your school board and patrons that you have been able to positively influence student outcomes. ■

References

Carnegie Council on Adolescent Development. (1989). *Turning points: Preparing American youth for the 21st century.* New York: The Carnegie Corporation.

Erb, T. O., & Stevenson, C. (1999a). What difference does teaming make? *Middle School Journal, 30* (3), 47-50.

Erb, T. O., & Stevenson, C. (1999b). Fostering growth inducing environments for student success. *Middle School Journal, 30* (4), 63-67.

Evertson, C. M., Weeks, K. W., & Randolph, C. H. (1996, August). *Creating learning-centered classrooms: Implications for classroom management.* Paper written for the Blue Ribbon Schools Program, Office of Educational Research and Improvement, Washington, DC.

Felner, R. D., Jackson, A. W., Kasak, D., Mulhall, P., Brand, S., & Flowers, N. (1997). The impact of school reform for the middle years: A longitudinal study of a network engaged in *Turning Points*-based comprehensive school transformation. *Phi Delta Kappan, 78,* 528-532, 541-550.

Flowers, N., Mertens, S. B., & Mulhall, P. F. (1999). The impact of teaming: Five research-based outcomes. *Middle School Journal, 31* (2), 57-60.

Flowers, N., Mertens, S. B., & Mulhall, P. F. (2000). What makes interdisciplinary teams effective? *Middle School Journal, 31* (4), 53-56.

Gehrke, N. J. (no date [1996, August]), *In search of the better school curriculum.* Paper written for the Blue Ribbon Schools Program, Office of Educational Research and Improvement, Washington, DC.

Jackson, A. W., & Davis, G. A. (2000). *Turning points 2000: Educating adolescents in the 21st century.* New York: Teachers College Press.

Lipsitz, J., Mizell, M. H., Jackson, A. W., & Austin, L. M. (1997). Speaking with one voice: A manifesto for middle-grades reform. *Phi Delta Kappan, 78,* 533-540.

National Middle School Association. (1982). *This we believe.* Columbus, OH: Author.

National Middle School Association. (1992). *This we believe.* Columbus, OH: Author.

National Middle School Association. (1995). *This we believe: Developmentally responsive middle level schools.* Columbus, OH: Author.

Schwab, J. J. (1973). The practical 3: Translation into curriculum. *School Review, 81,* 501-522.

Slavin, R. E. (1999). *Technical proposal: Design, development, and testing of comprehensive school reform models.* Baltimore: Success for All Foundation.

Stevenson, C., & Erb, T. O. (1998). How implementing *Turning Points* improves student outcomes. *Middle School Journal, 30* (1), 49-52.

2. Educators committed to young adolescents

C. Kenneth McEwin, & Thomas S. Dickinson

The most important quality middle school teachers bring to their classrooms is their commitment to the young adolescents they teach. Without this commitment there is little substantive progress for either party, and teaching and learning is reduced to some lifeless and mechanical act, the consequences of which fall most heavily on the young adolescents, their families, and ultimately the nation. Teachers who are committed to their students, however, breathe life and opportunity into their classrooms and into the future of the youth with which they work.

The Duality of Commitment

"Educators committed to young adolescents" (National Middle School Association, 1995, p. 13) are characterized by two equally important aspects of their commitment:

1. The provision of "significant academic learning experiences" (p. 13) for young adolescent students, learning experiences that are characterized by high content and high expectations for all learners.
2. The provision of developmentally appropriate classrooms, schools, programs, and practices for all young adolescent students within the learning community.

The presence of significant learning experiences (high content and high expectations) within a developmentally appropriate, safe, and supportive school context is an identifiable characteristic of developmentally responsive middle schools. And while *This We Believe: Developmentally Responsive Middle Level Schools* (1995) is a policy document that establishes broad goals for the profession, these twin aspects of commitment are attainable, regardless of the specific characteristics of individual school communities.

> Effective middle level educators make a conscious choice to work with young adolescents. They understand the developmental uniqueness of young adolescents and are as knowledgeable about their students as they are about the subject matter they teach.

11

This duality of commitment (significant academic learning and developmentally appropriate contexts) has numerous implications for the roles of middle school teachers. Middle school teachers committed to the students they teach perform at least five specific roles: (a) student advocate, (b) role model, (c) supporter of diversity, (d) collaborator, and, (e) lifelong learner. As well, the duality of commitment has implications for the professional preparation of middle school teachers and for their continuing professional development focusing on refining and extending their knowledge, dispositions, and skills to perform these and related roles successfully.

The role of advocate

Being a student advocate is a complex, but essential, responsibility at the middle school level. This advocacy has two fundamental audiences – a readily recognizable external audience (e.g., parents, colleagues, administrators, and the wider community) and a less-well acknowledged internal audience made up of the young adolescents themselves. The role of student advocate revolves around the dual aspects of commitment: advocating for developmentally appropriate programs and practices within classrooms and schools and advocating for learning experiences that are "rich" (Arnold, 1993) in all their curricular and instructional aspects.

To advocate for young adolescents to external audiences calls for depth of knowledge about "the developmental uniqueness of young adolescents" (National Middle School Association, 1995, p. 13). Committed middle level educators use their position to help educate family members and others about the developmental realities of early adolescence while exploding some of the negative myths frequently associated with the age group.

In working with young adolescents themselves committed educators advocate for realistic assessments of where individuals are and where they are going. Committed teachers sustain young adolescents as they learn new skills, chart new avenues of growth, and confront the challenges and promises of life.

Role model

Teaching under relentless scrutiny is a fact of life for middle school teachers. Acting as a positive role model for youth during such examinations brings with it moral obligations. Being an appropriate role model takes several complementary thrusts in the middle school. Most visible is to model behaviors for young adolescent students.

The second aspect of being a role model for young adolescents in the classroom involves modeling relationships. Young adolescents learn how to affiliate with others by observing both peers and adults. The ways teachers cooperate with colleagues, their appreciation of differences, and their dispositions towards others speak volumes, often more powerfully than the planned curriculum of the moment. The third aspect of modeling for young adolescents involves a relatively new phase of teacher respon-

Middle level educators also serve as role models for their students.

sibility – modeling healthy development. In an age when risk factors abound for youth, the approach that teachers take to their own health and safety have become paramount. Can teachers and other educators effectively advocate particular positions in curriculum without living them visibly?

Supporter of diversity

Middle school teachers committed to their students are marked by their dedication and respect for the diversity inherent in middle school classrooms. This implies both the traditional definitions of diversity (e.g., race, ethnicity, gender) and other facets such as developmental differences, learning styles, and exceptionalities. By being supporters of diversity in the classroom, committed middle school teachers embrace rather than reject "the needs, interests, and special abilities of their students" (National Middle School Association, 1995, p. 13).

— ■ —

Groups of students working outside the classroom itself – in halls, the common areas, the media center, or outdoors.

Collaborator

Being a committed middle school teacher means that professionally one is connected to members of the interdisciplinary team, to other teachers and teams throughout the building, and to administrators and support staff. Being a successful middle school teacher is a role that is characterized by a series of nested relationships.

Within individual classrooms there are connections to the team. These connections are about the students the team has in common, the curriculum intersections that characterize the team's curriculum, and the instructional practices that support and sustain learning among students. Collaborating with colleagues calls for cooperation for student purposes – high achievement for all. But collaboration goes beyond the team because committed middle school teachers have an obligation to being part of programs at the grade and school level, whether these programs involve advisories, intramurals, clubs, or other aspects of the middle school learning environment.

Lifelong learner

A committed middle school teacher is a model of lifelong learning. This learning is widespread and continuous: new teaching materials and teaching techniques, new and emerging technologies that have impact in the classroom, new subject matter knowledge. As the knowledge explosion continues, committed middle school teachers, rather than complaining and acting like Luddites, read\experiment, travel, and study. Their lifelong learning stance takes them to seminars, formal coursework, travel, focused training and apprenticeships, adventures in individual study, and other learning opportunities.

Lifelong learners know that moving beyond their own immediate comfort zones as learners is important for themselves and their students. They also know that one does not just learn "things" but also develops an appreciation of the what and how behind the learning. They develop an understanding of how truly difficult some aspects of learning are and what it means to try and fail as well as to try and succeed.

Preparation for a Unique Commitment

Making conscious decisions to teach at the middle level and being dedicated to teaching young adolescents are very important beginning points for those entering the profession. It seems logical that these dedicated professionals would begin their careers well equipped with the specialized knowledge, skills, and dispositions needed to be successful in the challenging and rewarding world of teaching young adolescents. The sad truth is that many thousands of prospective teachers who make decisions to teach young adolescents find that specialized professional preparation programs which focus on teaching 10- to 14-year-olds are simply unavailable in their states. Further, they frequently learn that if they wish to have a career in middle level education, they must major in elementary education or in a content area or two in secondary education. Those who are

Students in groups working on projects in which individuals take on various roles to take advantage of their individual strengths.

When the time comes to end class, students don't rush out but continue in conversations.

not discouraged and select one of these options typically spend the vast majority of their professional preparation learning about teaching young children or focusing on teaching single subjects in senior high schools. Upon completion of these programs, they are awarded licensure to teach in the elementary and middle grades or the middle and senior high school grades (e.g., K-8, 6-12).

Malpractice in middle level teacher preparation and licensure

The fact that these preparation programs can be completed and licensure awarded without candidates receiving specific preparation for teaching young adolescents or even completing middle level field experiences serves as an example of the malpractice in which many teacher preparation programs and licensure agencies/professional practice boards are currently engaged. They are not promoting and protecting the rights of all young adolescents by guaranteeing that middle level teachers have demonstrated the specialized knowledge, skills, and dispositions needed to teach effectively. In many states, the message from teacher preparation institutions, licensure agencies/boards, and even the profession itself seems to be, "Anyone with any kind of professional teacher preparation can teach at the middle level. There is no specialization needed." As has been the case historically, the education and welfare of young adolescents and their teachers have been largely ignored and forgotten in the name of politics and administrative convenience (McEwin & Dickinson, 1996).

One major result of the unfortunate situation just discussed is that many middle level teachers, and other educators, frequently work intensely in well-intentioned ways that damage rather than enhance the quality of learning opportunities provided for young adolescents. This lack of match between intentions and appropriate behaviors rarely results from malice or a lack of caring, but rather is virtually always the result of a lack of knowledge that should have been a crucial part of professional preparation programs that focus directly and exclusively on teaching young adolescents.

Consensus on the need for specialized programs

There is a growing consensus regarding the importance of and need for specialized middle level teacher preparation. Advocacy for comprehensive specialized middle level courses, field experiences, and other program components that are considered essential for effective middle level teacher preparation

— ■ —

Visiting resource persons, administrators, or other volunteers are seen "teaching."

— ■ —

At times it is hard to tell if this vibrant classroom is one of art, literature, science, mathematics, or some other subject area.

is increasingly emerging from teacher educators, foundations, professional organizations, and other sources. There is also increasing support from middle level teachers regarding the importance of comprehensive, specialized middle level teacher preparation (Arth, Lounsbury, McEwin, & Swaim, 1995; Carnegie Council on Adolescent Development, 1989; DeMedio & Mazur-Stewart, 1990; Jenkins & Jenkins, 1991; McEwin & Dickinson, 1995, 1996; McEwin, Dickinson, Erb, & Scales, 1995; McEwin, Dickinson, & Hamilton, 1998; National Association of State Directors of Teacher Education and Certification, 1994; National Board for Professional Teaching Standards, 1994; National Middle School Association, 1991, 1996; Page, Page, Dickinson, Warkentin, & Tibbles, 1992; Scales & McEwin, 1994, 1996).

Essential program components

A solid consensus about the essential programmatic components that should be included in specialized middle level teacher preparation has also emerged (Dickinson & Butler, 1994; Jackson & Davis, 2000; McEwin & Dickinson, 1997; National Association of State Directors of Teacher Education and Certification, 1994; National Board for Professional Teaching Standards, 1994; National Middle School Association; 1996; Page, Page, Dickinson, Warkentin, & Tibbles, 1992; Southern Regional Education Board, 1998).

The following components represent those that are unique to the middle level program and do not include other elements which are essential to all teacher preparation programs (e.g., diversity, instructional technology). They are (a) a thorough study of early adolescence and the needs of young adolescents; (b) a comprehensive study of middle level philosophy and organization; (c) a thorough study of middle level curriculum; (d) an intensive focus on planning, teaching, and assessment using developmentally and culturally responsive practices; (e) early and continuing middle level field experiences in a variety of good middle level settings; (f) study and practice in the collaborative role of middle level teachers in working with colleagues, families, and community members; (g) preparation in two or more broad teaching fields; and (h) a collaborative teacher preparation partnership between faculty at middle level schools and university-based middle level teacher educators that is responsible for all aspects of a site-based middle level teacher preparation program (McEwin & Dickinson, 1996).

— ■ —

Students and teachers conversing about portfolios where evidences of student work show growth.

— ■ —

Upon entering a class students immediately begin a start-up activity without teacher direction.

Barriers to progress

If actions are to be taken to change the direction of teacher preparation and licensure for middle level educators, it seems important to identify the barriers that have prevented significant progress from occurring in the past so that these pitfalls can be avoided in future efforts. Some of these barriers are: (a) the unavailability of specially prepared middle level teachers; (b) the negative, stereotyped image of young adolescents; (c) the presence of too few advocates at teacher preparation institutions and state agencies; (d) the desire for flexibility in assignment of middle level teachers; (e) the public's lack of knowledge about appropriate middle level schooling; (f) teacher resistance to change; (g) problems, real or perceived, with other teacher preparation programs; and (h) the limited number of instructors in teacher preparation programs with a depth of middle level knowledge and experience (McEwin & Dickinson, 1997). These barriers should not discourage those advocating specialized middle level teacher preparation and licensure for they have been overcome in several states such as North Carolina and Georgia (McEwin & Dickinson, 1996).

Looking to the future

In large measure, the future success of young adolescents depends greatly upon the dedication and hard work of teachers and other educators who choose to teacher them and serve them in other important ways. Deliberate career choices and dedicated work alone, however, are not sufficient to guarantee that all young adolescents will have opportunities to achieve their full potentials. Teachers and other educators need access to professional preparation programs which provide them with the specialized knowledge, skills, and dispositions needed to be highly accomplished in their practice.

Agreeing that the specialized professional preparation of middle school educators is an important idea is not enough. Courageous steps need to be take by middle level educators, professional associations, accreditation agencies, and other stakeholders to develop and support specialized middle level professional preparation programs and the middle level licensure which supports and sustains them. Only when action is taken to significantly improve the professional preparation of all who teach and work with young adolescents will middle level schooling universally provide the high quality educational opportunities that are needed to assure successful futures for our nation's youth. ■

— ■ —

Students helping to plan a field trip in ways that make it evident they are valued members of the school community.

— ■ —

Students capturing happenings throughout the building on video that will be shown on the school's channel, getting a certain event on tape to be seen later, or preserving images for use by a teacher in a National Board for Professional Teaching Standards portfolio.

Observations provided by Marylin T. Leinenbach, Chauncey Rose Middle School, Terre Haute, Indiana.

References

Arnold, J. (1993). A curriculum to empower young adolescents. *Midpoints Occasional Paper 4* (1). Columbus, OH: National Middle School Association.

Arth, A. A., Lounsbury, J. H., McEwin, C. K., & Swaim, J. H., (1995). *Middle level teachers: Portraits of excellence.* Columbus, OH: National Middle School Association and Reston VA: National Association of Secondary School Principals.

Carnegie Council on Adolescent Development (1989). *Turning points: Preparing American youth for the 21st century.* New York: Carnegie Corporation.

DeMedio, D., & Mazur-Stewart, M. (1990). Attitudes toward middle grades certification: A national survey. *NASSP Bulletin, 74* (525), 64-71.

Dickinson, T. S., & Butler, D. (1994). The journey to the other side of the desk: The education of middle school teachers. In F. M. Smith & C. O. Hausafus (Eds.), *The education of early adolescents: Home economics in the middle school* (Yearbook of the American Home Economics Association) (pp. 183-191). Peoria, IL: Macmillan McGraw-Hill.

Jackson, A., & Davis, G. (2000). *Turning points 2000: Educating adolescents in the 21st century.* New York: Teachers College Press.

Jenkins, D. M., & Jenkins, K. D. (1991). The NMSA Delphi report: Roadmap to the future. *Middle School Journal, 22* (4), 27-36.

McEwin, C. K., & Dickinson, T. S. (1995). *The professional preparation of middle level teachers: Profiles of successful programs.* Columbus, OH: National Middle School Association.

McEwin, C. K., & Dickinson, T. S. (1996). *Forgotten youth, forgotten teachers: Transformation of the professional preparation of teachers and young adolescents.* Washington DC: Council of Chief State School Officers, Middle Grade School State Policy Initiative, Carnegie Corporation of New York.

McEwin, C. K. & Dickinson, T. S. (1997) Middle level teacher preparation and licensure. In J. Irvin (Ed.), *What research says to the middle level practitioner* (2nd ed., pp. 223-229). Columbus, OH: National Middle School Association.

McEwin, C. K., Dickinson, T. S., Erb, T. O., & Scales, P. C. (1995). *A vision of excellence: Organizing principles for middle grades teacher preparation.* Columbus, OH: National Middle School Association.

McEwin, C. K., Dickinson, T. S., & Hamilton, H. (1998). *National board certified early adolescence/generalist teachers' view on middle level teacher preparation.* Boone, NC: Appalachian State University.

National Association of State Directors of Teacher Education and Certification. (1994). *NASDTEC outcome-based standards and portfolio assessment: Outcome-based teacher education standards for the elementary, middle and high school levels.* Seattle, WA: Author.

National Board of Professional Teaching Standards. (1994*). Early adolescent/generalist standards for national board certification.* Washington, DC: Author.

National Middle School Association. (1991). *Professional certification and preparation for the middle level: A position paper of National Middle School Association.* Columbus, OH: Author.

National Middle School Association. (1995). *This we believe: Developmentally responsive middle level schools.* Columbus, OH: Author.

National Middle School Association. (1996). *National Middle School Association/NCATE-approved curriculum guidelines.* Columbus, OH: Author.

Page, F., Page, J., Dickinson, T. S., Warkentin, R., & Tibbles, A. (1992). 4000 voices. *Middle School Journal 24* (1), Insert.

Scales, P. C., & McEwin, C. K. (1994). *Growing pains: The making of America's middle school teachers.* Columbus, OH: National Middle School Association.

Scales, P. C., & McEwin, C. K. (1996). The effects of comprehensive middle level teacher preparation programs. *Research in Middle Level Education Quarterly, 19* (1), 1-21.

Southern Regional Education Board. (1998*). Improving teaching in the middle grades: Higher standards for students aren't enough.* Atlanta, GA: Author.

Original article appeared in the May 1997 issue of *Middle School Journal, 28* (5), 50-53.

3. Developing and Implementing a "Shared Vision"

Sue Swaim

In 1980 National Middle School Association began to develop its initial position paper. Entitled *This We Believe,* it was first released in 1982 and subsequently reprinted 12 times with well over 100,000 copies being distributed throughout the education community. It became probably the most widely cited statement about the education of young adolescents and was very influential in guiding the development of the fledgling middle school movement.

However, in 1994 NMSA's Board of Trustees knew it was time to reconsider its basic position paper. Changes had occurred over the past 15 years – relevant research, the cumulative experience of thousands of middle level practitioners, and vast societal changes – that affected the lives and the education of young adolescents. It became imperative that *This We Believe* be revisited and thoughtfully reconsidered if it were to continue to provide forward-looking guidelines for the continued development of middle level education.

Reconceptualizing middle level education was no easy undertaking. The committee formed to tackle this task brought a wide variety of knowledge and experience to the table. Intensive discussions and numerous drafts of a new position paper followed. These drafts were reviewed by a large number of active middle level educators for further refinement and comment. In the end, a subcommittee finalized the document that was unanimously approved by NMSA's Board of Trustees in September 1995.

This re-visioning of middle level education, now entitled *This We Believe: Developmentally Responsive Middle Level Schools,* fully expresses our association's beliefs and commitment to middle level education as we enter the 21st century. The document has taken on dual roles. First, it is a position paper that provides strong professional guidelines for the education of young adolescents. Second, it is a call for action directed to educators, parents, and community members who

> A developmentally responsive middle level school is guided by a vision. Research and practice over the past three decades provide middle level educators with a solid foundation that informs our vision of middle level education.

collectively are responsible for implementing effective middle level schools.

In response to the dual functions of this new position paper, *Middle School Journal,* beginning with the September 1996 issue, instituted a department entitled "This We Believe and Now We Must Act." During the next two and one-half years *Middle School Journal* published a series of articles designed to clarify the rationale for and meaning of the 12 characteristics of a developmentally responsive middle school contained in *This We Believe.* In addi-

Educators seek to provide schools that are joyful places where learning and learners are celebrated.

tion, these articles helped readers reflect on the practical implications of each characteristic. It is important to recognize that these characteristics delineated in the position paper and subsequently discussed in this series do not constitute a checklist for middle school development. Although each characteristic is important in and of itself, the significance of the 12 characteristics lies in the strength of their combined and interacting relationships. Building upon the strength of these relationships, NMSA has sought to reconceptualize developmentally responsive middle level schools. "Such schools will promote the growth of young adolescents as scholars, democratic citizens, and increasingly competent, self-sufficient young people who are optimistic about their future" (NMSA, 1995, p. 10).

Initially, the following six foundational characteristics were identified. These are conditions that ideally should be in place before appropriate program decisions are made.

- Educators committed to young adolescents
- A shared vision
- High expectations for all

- An adult advocate for every student
- Family and community partnerships
- A positive school climate

When educators have a *shared vision,* an observer might see, hear, or feel...

— ■ —

Teachers empowered in learning communities (e.g., interdisciplinary teams with advisories), in control of instructional time, and using the opportunity to develop programs unique to their students.

— ■ —

Common planning time in addition to individual planning time giving teachers in learning communities a regularly designated time to plan for meeting students' needs.

When these characteristics are operative, schools are in the best position to make stronger, more appropriate decisions regarding educational programs for young adolescents in the following six general areas.

- Curriculum that is challenging, integrative, and exploratory
- Varied teaching and learning approaches
- Assessment and evaluation that promotes learning
- Flexible organizational structures
- Programs and policies that foster health, wellness, and safety
- Comprehensive guidance and support services

(NMSA, 1995, p. 10-11)

Taken together, these characteristics reflect NMSA's "shared vision" of what developmentally responsive middle schools could and should be at this time. This chapter addresses the characteristic of "a shared vision" from the school's point of view.

In order for a middle school to be effective for young adolescents, all the stakeholders – students, teachers, administrators, board of education members, central office personnel, and community members – must collaboratively develop a common vision that can guide the ongoing development of that middle school. This shared vision becomes the foundation on which a successful middle school is built. Without a vision that is understood and supported by the stakeholders, middle level reform efforts will be seriously flawed from the onset. Fundamental changes, built upon what we know about the unique needs and characteristics of young adolescent learners, will not happen overnight. Everyone involved must understand that reality or change efforts are likely to be short-lived or implemented in name only. The changes needed to make middle schools more effective require new attitudes and new understandings about learning and the broader goals of education. Extensive professional development is also needed to equip teachers and other educators for success in the new endeavor. The foundations must be in place so that the changes will go beyond the typical entry level debate that focuses on such things as changing the school's name, grade configuration, length of the school day or year, or co-curricular activities. Although these are appropriate topics in the overall discussion, they cannot be the "heart" of the shared vision. The "heart" of the shared vision must focus on the nature and needs of young adolescent learners. We must continually strive to answer the question, *Is what we are doing best for our kids based upon what we know today about learning, teaching, and the needs of society?*

Developing a shared vision

A shared vision cannot be developed overnight. It takes time and considerable discussion to build a strong and enduring vision – one that reflects the very best we can imagine about all the elements of schooling, including student achievement, student teacher relationships, and community participation. Research and practice over the past three decades provide a wealth of information for the initial development process.

Many districts begin with the formation of a middle level task force. The task force is usually comprised of representatives from all the stakeholder groups who must work together if schools are going to grow and change as they must in this critical time. The task force process must be collaborative in nature and should begin to develop the ongoing educational partnerships among the stakeholders that are crucial to the long-term success of any school's program.

As young adolescent learners have many different learning styles so do the members of a task force. Therefore, extensive opportunities must be provided to enable task force members to build a common knowledge base and a consensus philosophy. This involves both individual study and give and take dialogue among members of the group.

In addition to NMSA's *This We Believe,* there are two other volumes in the required reading category: *Turning Points: Preparing American Youth for the 21st Century* (Carnegie Council on Adolescent Development, 1989) and *Turning Points 2000: Educating Adolescents in the 21st Century* (Jackson & Davis, 2000). Additional resources such as Stevenson and Carr's (1993) *Integrated Studies in the Middle Grades: Dancing Through Walls* and research reports found through ERIC searches or NMSA's *Research in Middle Level Education Annual* are worthwhile. Most importantly shared literature study plus ample discussion and question and answer sessions must be a part of the information-gathering and digesting process.

Seeing something in action is also an important part of the development process. Visiting schools with strong middle level programs in place is especially valuable. However, before embarking on school visits, it is important to be clear about

— ■ —

The school improvement plan reflects the school's mission statement.

— ■ —

The large school population has been reduced into several extended families or learning communities, thereby improving student-teacher relationships and student achievement.

23

what the visitation team needs to see. Be specific about what you are seeking, ask for time not only to see such programs in action but to visit with teachers, administrators, parents, and students about what is happening in that school. Visitation teams should consist of representatives of all the stakeholder groups. This enables people to see and experience things from different viewpoints, continue their discussions upon return, and be responsive to the various constituencies each person represents.

Likewise, attending middle level conferences and workshops provides opportunities for people to confer with others in the field and to directly benefit from others' experiences and ideas. Ideally, the district will facilitate teams of stakeholders to attend these events. This enables several representatives to hear the same message at the same time, ask questions of the leaders, and return to school to continue discussion and follow-up exploration. All of these activities give the task force an opportunity to develop a common knowledge base and set of questions that must be addressed within its own community to help middle schools become all that they should and can be.

A task force must reach out to involve the community in the process. Identify key people in the community who have a direct interest in early adolescence such as pediatricians or other health professionals, youth club leaders, social workers, juvenile law enforcement personnel, or religious leaders. As important opinion leaders they can become resource people when addressing the community expectations for the middle school and help to articulate the vision throughout the community.

Ongoing communication is vitally important. Key issues or questions being studied by the task force must be clearly articulated to the community. The needs of young adolescents, how developmentally appropriate middle schools can lead to improved academic achievement, and financial considerations are among topics that must be addressed.

A planned program to disseminate information must be initiated. A variety of formats may be used such as guest speakers at highly publicized public meetings, school leaders speaking at civic organizations, special briefings for reporters and editors, school district policies and papers disseminated to parents, coffees hosted by principals, and open forums for community input. Teachers, parents, and even students should be directly involved in these events along with administrators, for they are parts of the key educational partnership needed to make the shared vision become reality.

— ■ —

The daily bulletin includes an announcement about the upcoming staff development programs on technology and curriculum integration.

— ■ —

Data measuring student outcomes are being collected and analyzed regularly to determine if programs and practices are increasing student success.

Implementing a shared vision

Once an overall vision for middle level education has been developed and articulated by the district, each middle level school needs to begin creating its own mission statement. The mission statement, of course, takes into account the district's philosophy and goals as well as relevant state guidelines. However, each school's mission statement should be "personalized" and unique to its own situation. Once again, all stakeholders should actively participate in the process of formulating a mission statement that will guide the school's new course. The mission statement should be very succinct and reflect the top priorities and beliefs of each school.

The clear challenge is to provide a rigorous and relevant education based on the developmental needs of young adolescent learners.

Most importantly, the mission statement must become a "living" one that readily guides specific decisions about programs and practices. When a mission statement becomes operational, middle level educators have a standard by which to judge those practices that will best provide the desired challenging, academic program. Too often mission statements are quickly developed by a relative few, approved routinely by a faculty, and, therefore, remain as rhetoric. An operational mission statement, however, is constantly being used and is also revisited as circumstances change, as the school community grows and learns through doing, and as new research and practices emerge.

An operational mission statement constantly raises the question, *Is what we're doing the best for our kids?* Without a shared vision and a mission statement that is understood and supported by all the stakeholders, a sense of aimlessness may prevail and limited harmony exist. Contradictory policies may coexist, and school supporters will not be able to take a lead. Uninformed and uninvolved people open the door to criticisms of the school, especially if a change takes place without adequate understanding. Ultimately, the sincere efforts and hard work of those involved can be undermined.

— ■ —

There is a sense that all teachers, staff, and administrators are "pulling the cart" in the same direction in an attempt to make a good school even better.

Communicating the shared vision and mission

One of the most important aspects of developing and implementing a shared vision and the related mission statement is how these are communicated to the wider audiences who also need to hear the message. Three important audiences are: (1) elementary and high school staffs, including support personnel; (2) all parents; and (3) the community at large, including its news media, business leaders, civic organizations, and religious leaders. The importance of developing a planned, ongoing communication program must not be overlooked. These audiences need to understand the rationale for middle level education as set forth in *This We Believe* and become familiar with the characteristics of this age group. They need to see how putting the shared vision and mission statement into action will increase student achievement and better meet the other developmental needs of 10-14 year olds. These are important issues and need to be addressed on an ongoing basis to all audiences if the support needed to achieve the best education possible for young adolescents in the community is going to be present.

Observations provided by David L. Nizinski and Bonnie J. Eaves, White Pine Middle School, Saginaw, Michigan.

NMSA's Call for Action

This We Believe set forth the challenge in these strong statements.

Educators, parents, and community members are urged to forge new and meaningful partnerships in order to transform *This We Believe* into a living document. It is time to launch those initiatives not yet begun, to strengthen those now underway, and for all stakeholders to re-dedicate themselves to the work needed to ensure the realization of these ideas and ideals.

The importance of achieving developmentally responsive middle level schools cannot be underestimated. The nature of the educational programs young adolescents experience during this formative period of life will, in large measure, determine the future for all of us. (p. 33)

This call to action that comprises the last two paragraphs in the position paper will require those of us directly involved in middle level schools to take the initiative. As professionals, we must assume leadership in bringing *This We Believe* to the attention of superintendents, board members, and parents. Needed discussion of the 12 characteristics, not only in individual school faculties but with parents and citizens, will not occur if we do not take the lead. The document has given us a valuable tool, but putting it into use will require action on our part. ■

References

Carnegie Council on Adolescent Development. (1989). *Turning points: Preparing American youth for the 21st century.* New York: Carnegie Corporation.

Jackson, A. W., & Davis, G. A. (2000). *Turning points 2000: Educating adolescents in the 21st century.* New York: Teachers College Press.

National Middle School Association. (1995). *This we believe: Developmentally responsive middle level schools.* Columbus, OH: Author.

Stevenson, C., & Carr, J. F. (1993). *Integrated studies in the middle grades: Dancing through walls.* New York: Teachers College Press.

Original article appeared in the September 1996 issue of *Middle School Journal, 28* (1), 54-57.

4. High Expectations for All

John Arnold

Educators in developmentally responsive middle level schools hold and act upon high expectations for all students, and the students themselves have expectations of success....
Successful middle level schools are grounded in the understanding that young adolescents are capable of far more than adults often assume.

olding high expectations for all — a phrase used so loosely in education circles that its crucial meanings and implications are frequently lost. Sometimes the phrase refers to little more than abstractly "raising standards," without enabling students to meet them. This procedure is akin to raising the cross bar for a high jumper without heeding the athlete's need to develop the technique and determination to clear the new height. In other instances, "holding high expectations" is limited to admonitions about improving students' standardized test scores or behavior, accompanied by strategies for teaching to tests or firming up discipline. The intentions of the section on holding high expectations in *This We Believe: Developmentally Responsive Middle Schools* (National Middle School Association, 1995) go far beyond these interpretations. They involve seeing and appealing to the best in young adolescents in all their diversity and in promoting ways to help them realize their potential in every realm of development. This chapter will elaborate these intentions and their implications.

It is well documented that expectations relative to students become self-fulfilling prophecies. Positive expectations promote positive attitudes and motivation to achieve; negative expectations lead to alienation, discouragement, and lack of effort. In the classic *Pygmalion in the Classroom* study (Rosenthal, 1968), teachers were assigned groups of students with similar IQs and past school performances. However, some teachers were told that their students had high IQs while other teachers were not told this. Students in the supposed high IQ groups outperformed the other students by a significant margin. In studies cited by George (1988) and Wheelock (1994), students with the same abilities tended to regard themselves and their peers as "dumb" if placed in a "low" group but "smart" if placed in a "high" group. Teachers' curriculum strategies differed markedly depending upon their perceptions of student ability. Clearly, adult expectations have a profound effect upon students' performances and attitudes.

The importance of positive expectations is magnified with regard to young adolescents because of the negative stereotypes which abound about them in our society. Popular wisdom regards them to be innately full of storm and stress, opposed to adult values, dominated by peer opinion, and uninterested in any intellectual concerns. As I have elaborated elsewhere (Arnold, 1993), this characterization is demonstrably untrue and highly destructive. While early adolescence is a difficult time for some, it is surely not unduly so for the majority. Studies show that young adolescents exhibit no more neurotic behavior than any other age group (Peterson, 1987), choose friends whose parents' values are consonant with those of their parents (Bandura, 1982), rely on significant adults in making important decisions (Lamb, Ketterlinus, and Fracasso, 1992), and are intellectually curious and alert (Keating, 1990). Predominant negative stereotypes are based largely on media images and psychiatric accounts of disturbed youth. They fail to realize that while puberty is undeniably a biological phenomenon, "adolescence" as we know it today is to a great extent the result of social forces that have increasingly isolated young people from the adult world and have created a youth culture. The starting point for high expectations and developmentally responsive middle schools, then, is ridding ourselves of negative stereotypes about young adolescents.

Beyond ridding ourselves of negative images, it is crucial to realize that given the opportunity and support, young adolescents are capable of far more than most of us imagine. To cite but a few examples, students in Alan Haskivtz' seventh grade class at Suzanne Middle School, a large Los Angeles County school that is some 60% Mexican American, proposed legislation that enables California to save billions of gallons of water annually; persuaded the county sheriff on the need to fingerprint all area children so that runaways and kidnapped children could be traced more easily; and helped the county registrar rewrite voter instructions when they discovered those at the polls were written on a college level of readability (Arnold, 1990).

In Sam Chattin's seventh grade science classroom in William H. English Middle School, Scottsburg, Indiana, students run the largest animal refuge shelter in the midwest. While nursing animals back to health, they study about living creatures, environmental policies, and a host of other biological issues. They have shared their work and insights through presenta-

When educators have *high expectations for all,* an observer might see, hear, or feel...

—■—

Volunteers active in school projects and in sharing talents with students.

—■—

Administrators meeting regularly with teams to discuss individual student growth and development.

—■—

Students' body language and facial expressions reveal they are relaxed and happy.

29

tions in ten states and as special guests of the International Animal Rights Convention in Tblisi, Russia (Arnold, 1990).

Over the past 20 years, seventh and eighth grade students of Erick Mortensen and Larry O'Keefe in the Paradise Project at Edmunds Middle School, Burlington, Vermont, have traveled an average of 40,000 miles a year. All details of each trip are planned and carried out by students, and twice yearly they publish a literary journal about their learning adventures. Further, they engage in an "achievement program," learning practical skills and teaching them to one another. To advance to level six of this Boy Scout-type program, one student organized a weekend cleanup of the Lake Champlain waterfront that mobilized some 1,000 citizens; another student made all arrangements for a month's stay in the school by a blind artist-in-residence. It is noteworthy that in all three of these examples, students' test scores have skyrocketed, though test scores have not been the focus of attention (Arnold, 1990).

As these examples indicate, if high expectations are to be realized, we must *empower* students to become intellectually engaged, to develop skills, to be responsible citizens who put forth sustained effort. Our concern must encompass their social, psychological, and moral development as well as their academic growth.

Owing to developmental diversity and individual differences, holding high expectations can seldom mean having the same expectations for all students. A developmentally responsive approach to teaching and learning necessarily implies one that is differentiated and personalized, taking into account individual needs, interests, and abilities. Such an approach is characterized by

- **Starting where students are, gearing instruction to their levels of development and understanding.** In virtually every middle level classroom, there will be many students who have limited capacity for complex, abstract reasoning, some who are comfortable with it, and a majority who are somewhere in transition from concrete to more abstract modes of thinking. To deal with this spectrum, teachers must be keen observers who provide a rich variety of materials, opportunities for hands on and experiential learning, and tasks which appropriately "stretch" students towards the next level.
- **Varying degrees of structure.** Some students will need at least initially, very explicit, straightforward assignments; others can handle choices from a limited menu;

—■—

The school climate is warm, inviting, and electric because of the positive things going on.

—■—

Students are encouraged to help others and are engaged in academic studies related to the service learning projects they are conducting this year.

others will be capable of initiating projects on their own. The aim is to move students as they are able towards increasing autonomy.

- **A varied pace of learning.** A friend recently commented, "In business, we expect employees to do high quality work, but vary the time needed to accomplish it. In education, you seem to vary the quality, but hold time constant." Where learning is self-paced or the amount of time students have to complete certain assignments is flexible, students are often able to improve the quality of their work considerably.

- **A variety of teaching/learning strategies.** Multiple approaches that involve whole groups, small groups, and individuals are needed to meet the different learning styles and types of intelligences that exist in middle level classrooms. In general, most effective strategies are activity-oriented and inquiry-based. They include integrative learning, cooperative learning, independent study, peer tutoring, direct instruction, service learning, apprenticeships, and a host of other approaches.

- **A curriculum that is rich in meaning, one that helps students make sense of themselves and their world.** Among other things, this implies that the content of what is studied deals with substantive issues and values, is related to students' own questions, opens doors to new learning, and is integrative in nature. Studies on alternatives to tracking (Oakes, 1985, Wheelock, 1994) indicate that curriculum rich in meaning enhances student performance at all levels.

- **Significant opportunities for students to assume initiative and responsibility with regard to curriculum and school life.** Where students are enable to make decisions and increasingly to take control of their own learning, motivation and achievement flourish. The common ingredient in the innovative programs described earlier is that students "own" the programs.

Quite obviously, it is a daunting task for teachers to develop many of these teaching/learning strategies. Yet if we hope to help students fulfill our high expectations, we must have them for ourselves as well. By learning one or two new methodologies a year, competent, committed teachers can build substantial repertoires over time. Also, it is important to note that effective teaming can greatly assist teachers in their professional growth. Where teams discuss and assess students systematically,

—■—

Teachers at lunch are heard talking about the neat kids they teach and how their students' ideas get translated into activities.

—■—

Team and exploratory teachers meet periodically to discuss student interests and to plan collaborative curriculum projects.

—■—

Students often lead all-team meetings.

they can learn a great deal about adolescents' development, learning styles, backgrounds, and interests; where they collaborate on curriculum, they can learn new strategies and refine familiar ones that meet student needs. Colleagues who work closely together with the same students have a powerful support system and the opportunity to learn a great deal from one another.

In schools truly responsive to young adolescents, the holding of high expectations is not limited to views about students. Administrators and parents, as well as teachers, hold high expectations for themselves and for one another. Adults as well as children respond positively to high expectations. It is well known that effective principals are essential to successful schools, doing much to set the tone, promote positive relationships, and keep the focus on student development and learning. Where principals have high expectations of teachers and support them in their efforts, teachers are much more likely to respond to students in a similar manner.

With regard to parents, educators in developmentally responsive schools understand that virtually all parents want their children to be successful and approach parents from this perspective. They are aware that parental attitudes toward learning greatly influence student progress, and that a partnership between home and school is necessary. As the work of Comer, Haynes, Joyner, and Ben-Avie (1996) has shown, this partnership is especially important relative to minority students. Impressive gains have been made where parents are incorporated into the goal-setting process for schools, faculty are helped to understand students needs, and parents are taught to support the learning process.

Holding high expectations for all and translating them into meaningful actions is surely not a simple task. It is an ongoing effort that changes and grows as we have new challenges and have fresh insights. As in all aspects of middle level education, the key lies in keeping our eye on the prize: the growth and development of young adolescents. Stevenson (1992) poignantly and powerfully reminded us of this potential:

> [My middle school teaching experience] has left me with immutable optimism about the potential of young adolescent children. Given learning opportunities that truly challenge, the responsibility to exercise meaningful choice, and respect for their ideas and dignity, youngsters are capable of tremendous

---

— ■ —

Students frequently talk to one another about their academic work.

— ■ —

High attendance rates, few tardies, and minimal disciplinary problems indicate that students want to be in school.

— ■ —

The teachers' lounge is empty.

Observations provided by Martha Hill, Northview Middle School, Hickory, North Carolina.

Young adolescents are curious and concerned about themselves and their world.

commitment and dazzling originality. Underneath the confounding, frustrating, often exhausting surface, there lies an indomitable human spirit, capable of the exceptional. (pp. 331-332)

Holding high expectations is not an empty exhortation. It is the bedrock of our efforts to create schools that truly honor young adolescents; schools that help them to become all that they can be. ■

References

Arnold, J. (1990*). Visions of teaching and learning: 80 exemplary middle level projects.* Columbus, OH: National Middle School Association.

Arnold, J. (1993) A curriculum to empower young adolescents. *Midpoints Occasional paper 4* (1). Columbus, OH: National Middle School Association.

Bandura, A. (1982). The stormy decade. Fact or fiction? In R. Grinder (Ed.) *Studies in adolescence*. London: Collier-McMillan.

Comer, J., Haynes, N., Joyner, E., & Ben-Avie, M. (Eds.). (1996). *Rallying the whole village: The Comer process for reforming education*. New York: Teachers College Press.

George, P. S. (1988). Tracking and ability grouping. *Middle School Journal, 20* (1), 21-28.

Keating, D. (1990). Adolescent thinking. In S. S. Feldman and G. I. Elliot (Eds.). *At the threshold: The developing adolescent* (pp. 54-89). Cambridge, MA: Harvard University Press.

Lamb, M., Ketterlinus, L., & Fracasso, M., (1992). Parent-child relationships. In M. Bornstein & M. Lamb (Eds.), *Developmental psychology: An advanced textbook* (pp. 465-518). Hillsdale, NH: Lawrence Erlbaum.

National Middle School Association. (1995*). This we believe: Developmentally responsive middle level schools.* Columbus, OH: Author.

Oakes, J. (1985). *Keeping track: How schools structure inequality.* New Haven, CT: Yale University Press.

Peterson, A. (1987, September). Those gangly years. *Psychology Today, 21,* 28-34.

Rosenthal, R. (1968). *Pygmalion in the classroom: Teacher expectations and pupils' intellectual development.* New York: Holt, Reinhart and Winston.

Stevenson, C. (1992). *Teaching ten to fourteen year olds.* White Plains, NY: Longman.

Wheelock, A. (1994). *Alternatives to tracking and ability grouping.* Alexandria, VA: Association for Supervision and Curriculum Development.

Original article appeared in the January 1997 issue *of Middle School Journal, 28* (3), 51-53.

5. Advisory: Advocacy for Every Student

Ross M. Burkhardt

Mr. B., I got a 93 on my test! Marisa rushed into my room between second and third periods to tell me the good news. For several weeks we had been discussing her lack of success in math. An honor student in seventh grade, Marisa was suddenly earning C's and D's on her eighth grade algebra tests. She was considering a tutor or possibly dropping to a lower ability level; recently she had begun attending math extra-help sessions. In my dual roles as Marisa's advisor and teacher, I saw her four times daily – morning advisory, social studies, lunch, and English. Once a month I had a 40-minute advisory conference with Marisa to discuss school and life in general. An accomplished actress who also enjoyed playing lacrosse, Marisa regularly shared with me the joys and woes of being thirteen; math was one of her burdens. I listened sympathetically as she voiced her frustrations (she knew that I was interested in her eventual success), and I suggested extra-help sessions. That is about all I did. Marisa did the rest.

This We Believe asserts that developmentally responsive middle level schools are characterized by, among other things, "an adult advocate for every student" (NMSA, 1995, p. 16). Why adult advocacy? What is it? And why is it important that the adults who teach middle level students also act as their advocates? Why should "each student [have] one adult who knows and cares for that individual and who supports that student's academic and personal development" (p. 16)?

Advocating for young adolescents is necessarily problematic as they navigate the transition from elementary to middle school, as their bodies grow and change, as they develop new interests and new peer groups, as they probe boundaries and test limits, as they explore a rapidly changing world via the Internet, as they consume a daily bombardment of advertising on television and in magazines, as they consider the varied messages embedded in the lyrics and music of current popular artists, as they confront sensational headlines, and as

> Each student has one adult who knows and cares for that individual and who supports that student's academic and personal development....This designated advocate must be a model of good character and be knowledgeable about both young adolescent development and middle level education.

When there is an *adult advocate for every student,* an observer might see, hear, or feel...

— ■ —

An advisory group seated in a circle discussing issues and concerns important to young adolescents.

— ■ —

Students eating lunch with advisors, sharing stories, solving problems, and catching up on overdue assignments as they share a safe place to hang out.

they edge tentatively, yet inexorably, towards maturity. Some emerging adolescents weather the turbulence with few upsets; others inhabit self-centered lives redolent with roller-coaster drama; still others experience pain and suffering resulting from abusive settings or unhealthy choices, or both. Clearly, educating today's youth is as great a challenge as it ever has been.

Many middle level schools respond to the question of advocacy by instituting advisory programs, also known as *Advisor/Advisee, Prime Time,* or *Home Base.* Whatever they are called, most advisory programs share several common attributes: a designated staff member responsible for a small group of students; regularly scheduled meetings of the advisory group; ongoing individual conferences between the advisor and the advisees during the school year; administrative support for advisory activities; parent contact with the school through the child's advisor; and, most importantly, an adult advocate for each young adolescent.

According to *This We Believe,* the obligation of a developmentally responsive middle level school is to provide "a continuity of caring that extends over the student's entire middle level experience so that no student is neglected" (NMSA, 1995, p. 17). An advisory program enables such a "continuity of caring" to take root. Schools that have instituted and maintained successful advisory programs note increased academic achievement, less vandalism, greater attendance, fewer alienated students, more student-centered learning, and a better climate permeating the building.

In 1989 the Carnegie Corporation, in its landmark publication *Turning Points: Preparing American Youth for the 21st Century*, presented eight recommendations for transforming the education of young adolescents and middle grade schools. The first recommendation endorsed the creation of smaller communities of learning; it also called for an adult advisor for each student. "The effect of the advisory system," noted the report, "appears to be to reduce alienation of students and to provide each young adolescent with the support of a caring adult who knows that student well. That bond can make the student's engagement and interest in learning a reality" (Carnegie Council on Adolescent Development, 1989, p. 41). That recommendation was reaffirmed in *Turning Points 2000: Educating Adolescents in the 21st Century* (Jackson & Davis, 2000). In 1981, Joan Lipsitz, then engaged in research for her acclaimed book, *Successful Schools for Young Adolescents,* encountered that phenomenon – the absence of alienation – at Shoreham-Wading River Middle School when she was told by a seventh grade girl,

"They absolutely know me here" (Lipstiz, 1984). Would that every middle school student in every middle level school could make the same declaration!

That notion – students being known and knowing that they are known by the adults in the building – is at the heart of advocacy. The two most important jobs middle level educators have is to know the students they teach and to address their varied needs. The National Board for Professional Teaching Standards is unambiguous on this point: "Accomplished [middle level] generalists draw on their knowledge of early adolescent development and their relationships with students to understand and foster their students' knowledge, skills, interests, aspirations, and values" (National Board for Professional Teaching Standards, 1994, p. 9). If teachers expect students to be engaged learners, they must communicate to those students that they are cared for, respected, welcomed, and appreciated. Young adolescents need affirmation. They need support. They need to know that those who are charged with educating them are also concerned about them. Advisory programs could make that interest a reality.

And yet, some schools that initiated programs during the past two decades lost sight of that concern. Too many advisory programs foundered because advisory was seen as a curriculum to be covered rather than a relationship to be nurtured. And while it is more difficult to develop relationships than it is to conduct paper and pencil activities, one goal of every educator ought to be a more intimate school setting for students. Jim Burns (1998) recently observed

> We've learned over the years that our thinking of [advisory] as a time of day and a set place to do a certain routine set of activities just didn't work. It's very important to the school community that people talk and have relationships. Hopefully we're moving past advisory programs as just "ten minutes a day" kinds of things, and we're moving into something more meaningful. We're finding that it doesn't really matter when [schools] do [advisory] as long as the community is talking and people are getting to know one another.

In his seminal work, *A Middle School Curriculum: From Rhetoric to Reality,* Beane (1993) argued that "the central purpose of the middle school curriculum should be helping early adolescents explore self and social meanings at this time in their

— ■ —

A "peer rap room" facilitated by an adviser operating during lunch periods and after school with students talking to each other about any concern or problem that comes up.

— ■ —

All the advisory groups planning for the school-wide "March Madness" a Round Robin Kickball Tournament.

— ■ —

A new student being guided through the first day by a fellow student in his homebase group. Their pictures are taken and will appear with a brief interview in the next edition of the school newspaper.

lives" (p. 18). When teachers serve as advisors to sixth, seventh, and eighth graders, they receive daily, if not hourly, reminders of what it is like to be a young adolescent in today's fast-paced world. Through conversation and contact with their charges, teachers gain useful insights into early adolescence that they can then weave into the ongoing classroom experience over the course of the school year.

Young adolescents are concerned about issues other than school, and they need assistance in facing the future.

> Often, the predominant question teens have while trying to exist in the larger, more anonymous middle school is whether life is really worth living. If we want them to answer this question with "Yes, life is worth living," then we must find the ways and time to give them the personal attention and support they need to grow up as healthy people in both body and mind. Support must come before challenge to help young people grow. (Rubinstein, 1994, p. 26).

Advocacy programs that focus on the needs of young adolescents provide such attention and support. As the adage goes, "Kids don't care how much you know until they know how much you care."

Initiating a program

How to begin? One useful approach is to have a faculty committee frame a mission statement that describes the nature and purpose of the advisory program for the school. In 1973 a group of advisors at Shoreham-Wading River Middle School drafted the following passage, still employed more than a quarter of a century later as the basic definition of SWR's nationally recognized program:

> Advisory is essentially a comprehensive, school-oriented, one-to-one relationship between the advisor and the advisee for the purposes of communication and direction. Advisory enables each student to have an adult advocate in the school, a person who can champion the advisee's cause in student-teacher, student-administrator, and student-student interactions. (Shoreham-Wading River Middle School, 1973).

— ■ —

Advisors using one day a week to help students stay in control of their lives through such strategies as locker clean-up, notebook organization, goal setting, and homework check.

— ■ —

An advisor attending a student event in which one of her advisees is participating.

— ■ —

Two advisory groups competing against each other in a "Jeopardy"-like game to review before a major test.

Advisors need to know what is expected of them as they advocate for young adolescents. A staff committee can compose a list of responsibilities – a job description – for advisors in the program. Often among these tasks are taking attendance, disseminating school announcements, collecting lunch money, handling minor discipline issues, and communicating with the families of advisees. NMSA's position paper states that "the advocate is the primary person at the school with whom the family makes contact when communicating about the child" (NMSA, 1995, p. 17). Also, when teachers "make themselves available to counsel and advise students on a wide range of issues from academic progress to peer relationships to extra-curricular opportunities," they form "constructive relationships" which enable students to become better learners and more responsible citizens (National Board for Professional Teaching Standards, 1994, p. 9). Such relationships also provide teachers with "a window to see more sharply aspects of their students' character, values, interests, and talents that might otherwise be overlooked" (National Board for Professional Teaching Standards, 1994, p. 9-10).

How does a teacher learn to become an effective advisor? Staff development opportunities are helpful, especially when veteran advisors share their experience with beginning advisors. Also, a positive attitude leads to expertise developed over time. Jane Wittlock, a veteran middle school teacher and administrator at Shoreham-Wading River Middle School, responded to the question, "What kind of training should an advisor have?" in the following manner: "I don't think training could really help. If you don't love ten- to fourteen-year-olds initially, nothing could help you become an advisor. If you think this age group is truly special, then you'll be a good advisor" (Shoreham-Wading River Middle School, 1989). Her response emphasizes the attitudinal nature of advisory. It is not a program of monthly or weekly activities, nor is it a curriculum to be followed or "covered." Rather, advisory can best be described as a positive relationship between the advisor and the advisee.

A school's priorities show up in the master schedule. In order for effective advisor/advisee relationships to blossom, the schedule must allow time for advisory activities to occur. Group meetings, individual conferences, parent conferences, program evaluation – all of these will appear in the school calendar where there is a serious commitment to making advisory work.

When creating advisory groups, small numbers work best. If every teacher serves as an advisor, the load is shared evenly, and more students are better served. An ideal advisory group

— ■ —

A birthday lunch with a special treat being held for all sixth graders who have a birthday this month.

— ■ —

An advisory group planning and preparing materials for the next phase of its community service project.

— ■ —

An adviser assisting his students in preparing a petition that will seek to change a school policy.

contains ten to twelve students. Advocacy takes time, and the smaller the group size, the more effective the advisor can be.

Whether beginning an advisory program or evaluating one that has been in place for many years, it is useful to provide the staff with opportunities to discuss, design, and modify the operational aspects of the program. Faculty meetings can be devoted to this purpose. The following set of questions may prove helpful for purposes of discussion, design, implementation, clarification, evaluation, and direction.

1. What does the school's mission statement say regarding advocacy?
2. What does "advocacy" mean? What are its parameters?
3. What does the advisory program mission statement say?
4. What are the basic responsibilities of an advisor?
5. Who in the school will "manage and maintain" the advisory program?
6. How will advisory groups be formed?
7. When do advisors meet with advisees in groups? When do advisors meet individually with advisees?
8. How will issues of confidentiality be handled?
9. Who will mediate differences of opinion among advisors regarding the resolution of problems with students?
10. What happens when a student wants to switch from one advisory group to another?
11. Should advisory groups contain students all at the same grade level or at different grade levels?
12. Should the advisor continue with his/her advisees all through middle school, or should each student have a new advisor each year?
13. Should an advisee attend an advisor/parent conference?
14. What happens when parents want to meet with a teacher other than the child's advisor?
15. How and when will the advisory program be evaluated?

Ultimately, "an advisory system is a simple method that ensures that no secondary school (middle school, junior high school, or high school) student becomes anonymous" (Goldberg, 1998, p. 1). Anonymity leads to alienation; and, in the minds of some young people, a feeling of alienation sanctions antisocial behavior. Advocacy for all minimizes if not eliminates the number of students who fall through the cracks. Education has always been a "human" business, and an advisory program "will appeal to any middle, junior, or high school that wishes to em-

—■—

An advisor in the teachers' work room calling the parent of an advisee.

Observations provided by Lea Macdonald, Pleasantville Middle School, Pleasantville, New York

phasize personalization" (Goldberg, 1998, ix). The more humane and caring the school is, the more readily a strong sense of community will flourish.

Why adult advocacy? Because the roles and responsibilities of teachers call for it. As Rubinstein (1994) so eloquently maintained in *Hints for Teaching Success in Middle Schools,* "The most critical need for any person is to find meaning, purpose, and significance. In order to do this, that person must feel understood, accepted, and affirmed" (p. 26). Advocacy for young adolescents provides affirmation and acceptance at a critical time in their lives. It is an essential element of the developmentally responsive middle level school. After all, "the nature of the educational programs young adolescents experience during this formative period of life will, in large measure, determine the future for all of us" (NMSA, 1995, p. 33). ■

References

Beane, J. A. (1993). *A middle school curriculum: From rhetoric to reality* (2nd ed.). Columbus, OH: National Middle School Association.

Burns, J. (1998). *National Middle School Association 25th anniversary interview.* Las Cruces, NM: Author.

Carnegie Council on Adolescent Development. (1989) *Turning points: Preparing American youth for the 21st century.* New York: The Carnegie Corporation.

Goldberg, M. F. (1998). *How to design an advisory system for a secondary school.* Alexandria, VA: Association for Supervision and Curriculum Development.

Jackson, A., & Davis, G. (2000). *Turning points 2000: Educating adolescents in the 21st century.* New York: Teachers College Press.

Lipsitz, J. (1984). *Successful schools for young adolescents.* East Brunswick, NJ: Transaction.

National Board for Professional Teaching Standards. (1994). *Early adolescence/generalist standards for national board certification.* Washington, DC: Author.

National Middle School Association. (1995). *This we believe: Developmentally responsive middle level schools.* Columbus, OH: Author.

Rubinstein, R. E. (1994). *Hints for teaching success in middle school.* Englewood, CO: Teacher Ideas Press.

Shoreham-Wading River Middle School. (1989). *Advisory activities at Shoreham-Wading River Middle School.* Shoreham, NY: Author.

Shoreham-Wading River Middle School. (1973). *Advisory handbook.* Shoreham, NY: Author.

Original article appeared in the January 1999 issue of *Middle School Journal, 30* (3), 51-54.

6. School, Family, and Community Partnerships

Joyce L. Epstein

This We Believe, the position paper of National Middle School Association, discusses 12 characteristics of responsive middle level schools. The beliefs set high expectations for good people, good places, and good programs in the middle grades. They are presented as important goals to improve the quality of life in schools and the quality of education for all young adolescents.

One characteristic of a responsive middle level school is "family and community partnerships." This goal is on every list for school improvement, but few schools have implemented comprehensive programs of partnership. This chapter addresses three questions to help middle level educators move from their beliefs to action: (a) What is a comprehensive program of school-family-community connections in the middle grades? (b) How do family and community partnerships link with the other elements of an effective middle level school? (c) How can schools answer the call for action to develop and maintain productive programs of partnerships?

> Schools recognize and support families and community members as participants in school programs by encouraging their roles in supporting learning and honoring them as essential volunteers. Parent, families, and community members can enrich the curriculum and facilitate learning.

A Framework for a Comprehensive Program of Partnerships: Six Types of Involvement

For decades studies have shown that families are important for children's learning, development, and school success across the grades. Research is accumulating that extends that social fact by showing that school programs of partnership are important for helping all families support their children's education from preschool through high school. Left on their own, few families continue as active partners in the middle grades. Currently, few families understand the ins and outs of early adolescence, middle level education, school and community programs and activities available to their children, the school system, and other issues and options that affect students in the middle grades. Studies show that if middle level schools implement comprehensive and inclusive programs of partnership, *then* many more families respond, including those who would not become involved on their own. ·

What is a comprehensive program of partnerships? From many studies and activities with educators and families, I have developed a framework of six types of involvement that helps schools establish full and productive programs of school-family-community partnerships. This section summarizes the six major types of involvement with a few sample practices that may be important in the middle grades. Also noted are some of the challenges that must be met for good implementation of partnership practices and examples of the results that can be expected from each type of involvement in the middle grades.

Type 1 – Parenting

Type 1 activities assist families with parenting skills, understanding young adolescent development, and setting home conditions to support learning at each age and grade level. Other Type 1 activities help schools obtain information from families so that educators understand families' backgrounds, cultures, and goals for their children.

Sample practices. Among Type 1 activities, middle level schools may conduct workshops for parents; provide short, clear summaries of important information on parenting; and organize opportunities for parents to exchange ideas on topics of young adolescent development including health, nutrition, discipline, guidance, peer pressure, preventing drug abuse, and planning for the future. Type 1 activities also provide information in useful forms on children's transitions to the middle grades and to high school, attendance policies, and other topics that are important for young adolescents' success in school. Middle schools may offer parent education, family support programs, family computer classes, and other programs. To ensure family input, at the start of each school year or periodically, teachers may ask parents to share insights about their children's strengths, talents, interests, needs, and goals.

Challenges. One challenge for successful Type 1 activities is to *get information to those who cannot come to meetings and workshops at the school building.* This may be done with videos, tape recordings, summaries, newsletters, cable broadcasts, phone calls, computerized messages, school web sites, and other print and non-print communications. Another Type 1 challenge is to *design procedures that enable all families to share information about their children with teachers, counselors, and others.*

When *family and community partnerships* are in operation, an observer might see, hear, or feel...

— ■ —

An Action Team's plan guides the implementation of goal-oriented school, family, and community activities. Members are a diverse group representing parents, administrators, counselors, teachers, and community partners from such services as teen health, parks and recreation, juvenile justice, Boys and Girls Clubs, and Big Brothers and Big Sisters.

A workshop for parents and families scheduled on health and nutrition to both provide information and an opportunity for exchanging ideas and concerns.

Expected results. If information flows to and from families about young adolescent development, parents should increase their confidence about parenting, students should be more aware of parents' continuing guidance, and teachers should better understand their students' families. Specifically, if practices are targeted to help families send their children to school on time, then student attendance should improve. If families are part of their children's transitions from elementary to middle school and from middle to high school, more students should adjust well to their new schools, and more parents should remain involved across the grades.

Type 2 – Communicating

Type 2 activities communicate with families about school programs and student progress with school-to-home and home-to-school contacts such as notices, memos, conferences, report cards, newsletters, phone and computerized messages, the Internet, open houses, and other innovative communications.

Sample practices. Among many Type 2 activities, middle level schools may provide clear information on each teacher's criteria for report card grades, how to interpret interim reports, and, as necessary, how to work with students to improve grades. Type 2 activities include conferences for parents with teams of teachers, or parent-student-teacher conferences to ensure that students take personal responsibility for learning. Schools may organize class parents, block parents, or telephone trees for more effective communications and set up the equivalent of an educational welcome wagon for families who transfer to the school during the school year. Activities may be designed to improve school newsletters to include student work and recognitions, parent columns, important calendars, and parent response forms.

Challenges. One challenge for successful Type 2 activities is to *make communications clear and understandable for all families,* including parents who have less formal education or who do not read English

Regular school newsletters, student progress reports, parent-teacher conferences, telephone calls, and special bulletins are useful communications tools.

well, so that all families can process and respond to the information they receive. Other Type 2 challenges are to *know which families are and are not receiving the communications* in order to work to reach all families, *develop effective two-way channels of communication* so that families can easily contact and respond to educators, and *make sure that young adolescent students understand and participate in all school-family-community partnerships.*

Expected results. If communications are clear and useful and 2-way channels are easily accessed, home-school interactions should increase. More families should understand the school's programs, follow their children's progress, and attend parent-teacher conferences. Specifically, if computerized phone lines are used to communicate information about homework, more families should know more about their children's daily assignments. If newsletters include respond and reply forms, more families should offer ideas, questions, and comments about school programs and activities.

Type 3 – Volunteering

Type 3 activities improve recruitment, training, and schedules to involve parents and others as volunteers and as audiences at the school or in other locations to support students and school programs.

Sample practices. Among many Type 3 activities, middle level schools may collect information on family members' talents, occupations, interests, and availability to serve as volunteers to enrich students' subject classes; improve career explorations; serve as language translators; conduct attendance monitoring and phone calls; work on "parent patrols" for safety; organize and improve activities such as clothing and uniform exchanges, school stores, fairs, and many other activities. Schools may also create opportunities for mentors, coaches, tutors, and leaders of after-school programs to ensure that middle grades students have important and safe activities that expand their skills and talents. For Type 3, middle schools may establish a Family Center at the school where parents may obtain information, conduct volunteer work for the school, or meet with other parents (Johnson, 1996).

Challenges. Challenges for successful Type 3 activities are to *recruit volunteers widely so that all feel welcome, make hours flexible for parents and other volunteers who work during the school day, provide needed training, and enable volunteers to contribute productively* to the school, classroom curricula, and after-school programs at the school and in the com-

— ■ —

One-Year Action Plans tied to school improvement goals are being written. A look at a draft shows activities for all six types of involvement.

— ■ —

A subcommittee of the Action Team is meeting this afternoon according to an announcement in the daily bulletin.

munity. Volunteers will be better integrated into a school program if there is a coordinator who matches volunteers' times and skills with the needs of teachers, administrators, and students. Another Type 3 challenge is to *change the definition of "volunteer" to mean any one who supports school goals or students' learning at any time and in any place.* A related challenge *is to aid young adolescents in understanding how volunteers help their school, and to encourage students to volunteer themselves to help their school, family, and community.*

Expected results. If tasks, schedules, and locations are varied, more parents, family members, and others in the community should become volunteers to support the school and students. More will attend events, student performances, and activities as members of audiences. More families should feel comfortable and familiar with the school and staff, more students will talk and interact with varied adults, and more teachers should be aware of and use parents' and other community members' talents and resources to improve school programs and activities. Specifically, volunteer attendance monitors should alert families to help students improve attendance (Sanders, 1999). If volunteers conduct a "hall patrol" or are active in other locations, student behavior problems should decrease due to a better student-adult ratio. If volunteers serve as tutors for particular subjects, student tutees should improve their skills in that subject. If volunteers discuss careers, students should be more aware of their options for the future.

Type 4 – Learning at home

Type 4 activities involve families with their children in academic learning activities at home that are coordinated with students' classwork and that contribute to success in school. These include interactive homework, goal setting, and other curriculum-linked activities and decisions about academic courses and school programs.

Sample practices. Among many Type 4 activities, middle level schools may provide information to students and to parents about the skills needed to pass each course and each teacher's homework policies. Schools may also implement activities that help families encourage, praise, guide, and monitor their children's work using interactive homework, student-teacher-family contracts, long-term projects, summer home-learning packets, student-led conferences with parents at home about their writing, goal setting activities, homework hotlines of daily assignments, or other interactive strategies that keep students and families talking about schoolwork at home. (See

---

— ■ —

The Action Team's records show that most families participate in more than one activity planned by the Action Team each year.

— ■ —

At the end of the year, evaluations and celebrations take place to share best practices and to plan the partnership program for the next school year.

for example *Teachers Involve Parents in Schoolwork* (TIPS) by Epstein, Salinas, & Jackson, 1995).

Challenges. One challenge for successful Type 4 activities is to *implement a regular schedule of interactive work* that requires students to take responsibility for discussing with family members important things they are learning, interviewing family members, recording reactions, and sharing their work and ideas at home. Another Type 4 challenge is to *create procedures and activities that involve families regularly and systematically with students on short-term and long-term goal setting* for attendance, achievement, behavior, talent development, and future plans.

Expected results. If Type 4 activities are well designed and well implemented, students should improve their homework completion, report card grades, and test scores in specific subjects. More families should know what their children are learning in class and how to monitor, support, and discuss homework. Students and teachers should be more aware of family interest in students' work.

Type 5—Decision making

Type 5 activities include families in developing school vision and mission statements, and in designing, reviewing, and improving other policies and school decisions. Family members are participants on school improvement teams, committees, PTA/PTO or other parent organizations, Title I school and district councils, and advocacy groups.

Sample practices. Among Type 5 activities, middle level schools may organize and maintain an active parent association and include family representatives on all committees for school improvement such as curriculum, safety, supplies and equipment, partnerships, and career development. Schools may offer parents and teachers special training in leadership, decision making, and collaboration. Type 5 activities help to identify and prepare information desired by families about school policies, course offerings, student placements and groups, special services, tests and assessments, and annual results for students of their experiences and evaluations. In particular, family representatives, teachers, administrators, students, and community are members of the Action Team for School, Family, and Community Partnerships.

Challenges. One challenge for successful Type 5 activities is to *include in leadership roles parent representatives from all of the race and ethnic groups, socioeconomic groups, and geographic communities* that are present in the middle level

—■—

Interactive homework assignments in math let students demonstrate their skills for families and celebrate progress.

—■—

A framed certificate indicates that the school is a member of the National Network of Partnership Schools at Johns Hopkins University.

47

—■—

The School Improvement Team, Action Team for Partnerships, and PTA include parent representatives; and all work together to meet school improvement goals.

school. A related challenge is to *help parent leaders serve as true representatives* to obtain information from and provide information to all parents about decisions that are made. Another Type 5 challenge is to *include middle grades student representatives in decision-making groups* and leadership positions. An ongoing challenge is to *help parent and teacher members of committees to trust, respect, and listen to each other* as they work toward common goals for school improvement.

Expected results. If Type 5 activities are well implemented, more families should have input into decisions that affect the quality of their children's education, students should increase their awareness that families have a say in school policies, and teachers should increase their understanding of family perspectives on policies and programs for improving the school.

Type 6—Collaborating with the community

Type 6 activities coordinate the work and resources of community businesses; agencies; cultural, civic, and religious organizations; colleges or universities; and other groups to strengthen school programs, family practices, and student learning and development. Other activities enable students, staff, and families to contribute their services to the community

Sample practices. Among many Type 6 activities, middle level schools may inform students and families about the existence of programs and resources in their community such as after-school recreation, tutorial programs, health services, cultural events, service opportunities, and summer programs. This includes the need to design processes that increase equity of access for students and families to community resources and programs. Collaborations with community businesses, groups, and agencies also strengthen the other types of involvement such as conducting parent education workshops or meetings for families at community or business locations (Type 1); communicating about school events via local radio, TV, churches, clinics, supermarkets, and laundromats (Type 2); soliciting volunteers from businesses and the community and organizing activities such as "gold card" discount programs with local merchants (Type 3); enriching student learning with artists, scientists,

The school takes the initiative in providing a wide variety of opportunities for parent and community involvement.

writers, mathematicians, and others whose careers link to the school curriculum (Type 4); and including community members on decision making councils and committees (Type 5).

Challenges. One challenge for successful Type 6 activities is to *solve the problems associated with community/school collaborations* such as "turf" problems of funding and leadership for cooperative activities. Another Type 6 challenge is to *recognize and link students' valuable learning experiences in the community to the school curricula* including lessons that build on non-school skills and talents, and club and volunteer work. A major challenge is to *inform and involve the family* in community-related activities that affect their children.

Expected results. Well implemented Type 6 activities should increase the knowledge that families, students, and schools have about resources and programs in their community that could contribute to the attainment of important goals. Well-designed community connections should increase the equity of access to those opportunities for all students. Coordinated community services should help more students and their families solve problems that arise in early adolescence before they become too serious. Type 6 activities also should support and measurably enrich school curricula and extracurricular programs.

The six types of involvement create a comprehensive program of partnerships, but the implementation challenges for each type must be met in order for partnership programs to be effective. The results expected are directly linked to the design and content of the activities. Not every practice to involve families will result in higher student test scores. Rather, practices for each type of involvement can be selected to help students, families, and teachers reach specific goals or results. The summary above offers a few of hundreds of activities that can help middle schools build good partnerships. Details of middle level schools about the framework of six types of involvement, practices, challenges, and results are provided in Epstein (1995); Epstein, Coates, Salinas, Sanders, and Simon (1997); Epstein and Connors (1995); Palanki, Burch, and Davies (1995); Rutherford (1995); Sanders (1996), and Sanders (1999).

— ■ —

The school's budget shows a line for family and community partnerships.

Linking Partnerships to Other Recommended Middle Level Characteristics

The twelve characteristics of responsive middle levels schools in *This We Believe* are interrelated. Educators who want to work with young adolescents contribute to a shared vision that stipulates high expectations for all. The school program ensures high support with an adult advocate for every student and partnerships with all students' families and communities. Academically, the curriculum for each subject is challenging, integrative, and exploratory. Teachers use varied instructional approaches, assessments, and evaluations within a flexible instructional organization. Students are offered good guidance and programs that promote their health and safety. These elements must combine to promote all students' learning in a climate that is inviting, challenging, and joyful.

Each element also can be linked to all others. It is particularly important for middle level educators to understand how school-family-community partnerships are linked to other recommended elements so that parent involvement is not something extra, separate, or different from the "real work" of a school. There are several ways that family and community connections link with and promote the other recommendations in *This We Believe*.

—■—

The school uses active two-way channels of communication so teachers and parents can stay in touch.

Educators committed to young adolescents

To understand young adolescents, educators need to understand their students' families – their cultures, hopes, and dreams. In a good partnership program, families are helped to understand young adolescents, middle level schools, peer pressure, and other topics of importance and educators are helped to understand students' families. Indeed, middle level educators serve as role models for students by the way they talk about, talk with, and work with students' families. Many young adolescents are trying to balance their love for their family, need for guidance, and need for greater independence. Middle level educators who understand students' families can help students see that these seemingly contradictory pressures can coexist.

A shared vision

Along with educators and students, families and community members must contribute to the shared vision of a responsive middle level school. Structures, processes, and specific practices are needed that enable parents and community members to provide input to a new vision or mission statement and to periodic revisions of these documents. Vision and mission statements should be presented and discussed each year as new families and students enter or transfer to the middle level school.

High expectations for all

National and local surveys of middle grades students and their families indicate that they have very high expectations of success in school and in life. Fully 98% of a national sample of eighth grade students plan to graduate from high school; and 82% plan at least some post-secondary schooling, with 70% aiming to complete college (Epstein & Lee, 1995). Responsive middle level schools must incorporate students' and families' high aspirations into the school's high expectations for all. This means helping students take the courses they need to meet their goals and assisting students when they need extra time and help to learn by conducting coaching classes before and after school and on Saturdays, offering extra elective courses and summer classes, and using responsive practices.

An adult advocate for every student

School-based advocates and teacher advisors need to know each student's family. In some schools, students have the same advisor/advocate every year. This makes it possible for the advisor and students' families to get to know each other well. The advocate can serve as a key contact for the family should questions or concerns arise, facilitating two-way channels of communication before problems become too serious to solve.

Positive school climate

A safe, welcoming, stimulating, and caring environment describes a good school for students, educators, families, and the community. In a school with strong partnerships, family and community members are more likely to volunteer to help ensure the safety of the playground, hallways, and lunchroom; to share their talents in classroom discussions; and lead or coach programs after school to create a true school community.

Curriculum that is challenging, integrative, and exploratory

Families and communities need to know about all of the courses, special programs, and services that are offered to increase student learning in the middle grades. Good information about the curriculum helps families know that their children's schools are hard at work and helps families discuss important academic topics with their young adolescents. Families also need good information about how their students are progressing in each subject, how to help students set and meet learning goals, how to monitor and discuss homework, and how

In any partnership, all parties must benefit and have mutually understood roles and expectations.

to work with students to solve major problems that threaten course or grade level failure. Some middle level schools create student educational plans based on conferences with students and parents (Lloyd, 1996). If schools are serious about student learning, school-family-community partnerships must include information on and involvement with the curriculum.

Varied teaching and learning approaches

— ■ —

Some parents volunteer at school while others help in other ways.

Families need to know more about the varied instructional approaches that middle grades teachers use in all subjects, including group activities, problem-solving strategies, prewriting strategies, students as historians, hands-on science, and other challenging innovations that promote learning. Many new instructional approaches are unfamiliar to families so they may not understand the varied ways that students learn different subjects. Some instructional approaches can be designed to involve parents as does the Teachers Involve Parents in Schoolwork (TIPS) interactive homework process that asks students to share, show, and demonstrate not only what they are learning in class but how they are learning math, science, and language arts in the middle grades.

Assessments and evaluations that promote learning

Families and community members need to know about the major tests, new or traditional assessments, report card criteria, and other standards that schools use to determine children's progress and paths. In Maryland, for example, many schools conduct evening meetings for parents to learn about and try items on new performance-based assessments. Students and families also can help set learning goals and strategies for reaching goals. They can rate progress in parent-teacher-student conferences, on student self-report cards, and family-report cards. In Massachusetts, Project Write required students to share their writing portfolios with a parent and obtain reactions and suggestions. Middle grades educator Ross Burkhardt extended this family review by asking students to reflect on their families' reactions and then write about their own plans for improving their writing. Students and families also should have opportunities to rate the quality of school programs each year. There are many ways to include students and families in important assessments and evaluations in order to make those measures more meaningful.

Flexible organizational structures

Families need to understand "interdisciplinary teams" and "houses," schedules, electives or exploratories, and other arrangements that define middle level school organizations (Mac Iver & Epstein, 1991). Every middle level school should have annual group meetings and individual meetings of parents, teachers, and advisors to ensure that families understand how classes are organized and to gather family input for the decisions that affect their children's experiences and education.

Programs and policies that foster health and safety

Family responsibilities for their children's health and safety out of school are directly linked to what happens in school. Students, families, and community members must help develop and review safety policies, health policies, dress codes, lunch menus, facilities and equipment, and other policies and conditions that concern children's health and safety. If schools refer students for special services, families must be part of those decisions.

Comprehensive guidance and support services

Families need to know about formal and informal guidance programs at the school. This includes knowing the names, phone numbers, e-mail addresses, or voice-mail boxes of their children's teachers, counselors, advocates, or administrators in order to reach them with questions about their children's lives and work at school. In some middle level schools, guidance counselors are members of interdisciplinary teams and meet with teachers, parents, and students on a regular schedule and in other meetings as needed.

School-family-community partnerships must link with all of the elements of effective middle level schools to ensure that families remain important, positive influences in their young adolescents' education.

— ■ —

A sense of community can be felt at the school as parents, educators, students, and communitiy partners work in collaboration to help students succeed.

Observations provided by Geraldine Hill and Joyce Venable, Thurgood Marshall Middle School #170, Baltimore, Maryland, and Patricia Kidd-Ryce, Northeast Area Facilitator for School, Family, and Community Partnerships.

Call to Action: The National Network
of Partnership Schools

Most middle level educators want to build strong school-family-community partnerships, but most have not reached this goal. Indeed, developing good connections among homes, schools, and communities is an ongoing process that takes time, organization, and effort. Based on research and the work of many educators, parents, and students, I have initiated a program to help all elementary, middle, and high schools build positive, permanent programs of partnerships with families and communities.

Schools, districts, and state departments of education are invited to join the National Network of Partnership Schools at Johns Hopkins University to obtain assistance in improving school-family-community connections. There are no membership fees to join the National Network, but states, districts, and schools must meet a few requirements and invest in their own programs and staffs. Each Partnership School agrees to strengthen its program by using an action team approach and by addressing the six major types of involvement. Each school tailors its plans and practices for the six types of involvement to meet the needs, goals, and interests of its students, parents, and teachers. Each school starts with an inventory of present practices, develops a three-year outline, and writes a one-year action plan. District and state leaders are helped to organize their leadership activities to assist increasing numbers of schools to conduct these activities.

The National Network of Partnership Schools is not an "extra" program, but is part of every school improvement plan. To obtain an invitation and membership forms for schools, districts, or states, write to: Dr. Joyce L. Epstein, Director, National Network of Partnership Schools, Center on School, Family, and Community Partnerships, 3003 North Charles Street, Suite 200, Baltimore, MD 21218, or contact Karen Clark Salinas: tel: 410-516-8818 fax: 410-516-8890. ∎

References

Epstein, J. L. (1995). School/family/community partnerships: Caring for the children we share. *Phi Delta Kappan 76*, 701-712.

Epstein, J. L., Coates, L., Salinas, K. C., Sanders, M.G., & Simon, B. S. (1997). *School, family, and community partnerships: Your handbook for action.* Thousand Oaks, CA: Corwin Press.

Epstein, J. L., & Connors, L. J. (1995). School and family partnerships in the middle grades. In B. Rutherford (Ed.). *Creating family/*

school partnerships (pp. 137-166). Columbus, OH: National Middle School Association.

Epstein, J. L, & Lee, S. (1995). National patterns of school and family connections in the middle grades. In B. Ryan, G. Adams, T. Gullotta, R. Weissberg, & R. Hampton (Eds.), *The family-school connection. Theory, research and practice* (pp. 108-154). Thousand Oaks, CA: Sage.

Epstein, J. L., Salinas, K. C., & Jackson, V. (1995). *Teachers Involve Parents in Schoolwork (TIPS) language arts, science/health, and math interactive homework in the middle grades.* (Manual for teachers and prototype homework activities, grades 6, 7, & 8). Baltimore: Center on School, Family, and Community Partnerships.

Johnson, V. R. (1996). *Family center guidebook.* Baltimore: Center on Families, Communities, Schools and Children's Learning.

Lloyd, G. M. (1996). Research and practical applications for school, family, and community partnerships. In A. Booth & J. F. Dunn (Eds.), *Family-school links: How do they affect educational outcomes?* (pp. 255-264). Mahwah, NJ: Lawrence Erlbaum Associates.

Mac Iver, D. J., & Epstein, J. L. (1991). Responsive practices in the middle grades: Teacher teams, advisory groups, remedial instruction, and school transition program. *American Journal of Education, 99,* 587-622.

Palanki, A., & Burch, P., with Davies, D. (1995). *In our hands: A multi-site parent-teacher action research project. Report 30.* Baltimore: Center on Families, Communities, Schools and Children's Learning.

Rutherford, B. (Ed.) (1995) *Creating family/school partnerships.* Columbus, OH: National Middle School Association.

Sanders, M. G. (1996). Action teams in action: Interviews and observations in three schools in Baltimore school-family-community partnership program. *Journal of Education for Students Placed at Risk, 1* (3), 249-262.

Sanders, M. G. (1999). Improving school, family, and community partnerships in urban schools. *Middle School Journal, 31* (2), 35-41.

Original article appeared in the November 1996 issue of *Middle School Journal, 28* (2), 43-48.

7. A Positive School Climate

Marion Johnson Payne

> The climate of a developmentally responsive middle level school is safe, inviting, and caring; it promotes a sense of community and encourages learning. ... The climate encourages positive risk-taking, initiative, and the building of substantive relationships.

Developmentally responsive middle level schools are characterized by six defining conditions. One of these conditions, Positive School Climate, could well head the list, because creating the "right" atmosphere or environment in a school can make or break the entire school program. The development of a positive climate has its roots in the establishment of a shared vision. If all stakeholders have been involved in the birth and nurturing of the vision, then the foundation for a positive climate is in place.

What does a positive school climate look like? How does one determine that a positive school climate exists? How does a school maintain this positive climate? What pitfalls should be avoided?

The "looks" of a positive school climate

In a building where a positive school climate exists, there is a feeling of warmth. Banners, posters, and displays signal a sense of pride. Students, staff, and visitors feel they belong. Their sense of safety and security is not threatened. Attendance is high in such schools.

A positive climate affects student achievement. Students and teachers are empowered to take risks. Taking these risks ensures increased production, but it also fosters that essential critical thinking skill – problem solving. Students and teachers in a school with a positive school climate take pride in identifying and solving problems.

Determining the existence of a positive climate

A successful middle school is one that involves students, staff, parents, and the community in a partnership. In order to determine the climate of any school, all stakeholders should have been involved in the evaluation process. Three key conditions that are indicative of a positive climate are these.

- The environment promotes creativity, responsible risk taking, cooperation, and mutual trust and respect.
- Staff and students feel safe at school and in work-related activities.
- Staff, students, and parents all report that the learning environment is academically stimulating.

Good communication is vital in maintaining positive interactions within a school community. An excellent tool in evaluating any program is a survey that can be sent out at least annually to a random sample of school and community members.

Evidences of a positive school climate include but are not limited to the following items.

- Degree of community involvement (parents, volunteers, and community business partners)
- High daily attendance
- Positive attitudes of teachers, students, and parents
- A sense of ownership and pride in one's school
- High degree of participation in school-wide and system-wide activities
- Ability to spring back from a tragedy and become a stronger community
- Positive media relations and coverage
- Rigorous academic expectations for all students

The way in which a school handles an adverse situation is a strong indicator of that school's climate. One with a positive climate is able to approach each day and each situation as an opportunity for growth and community building. When faced with the sudden death of a student, Mount View Middle School in Marriottsville, Maryland, was forced to come together with the community and work through the tragedy.

From the onset of the tragedy, the school became a place to gather for comfort, information, planning, dialoguing, and grieving. Individuals in the community dealt with all the aspects of this traumatic experience. Throughout the week, staff members were given released time to either meet with a counselor or take time for themselves. A cadre of parents established a highly comforting presence and at the same time did not permit the media to interfere with the safe haven within. One family chartered a bus to provide transportation for any students who wanted to attend the funeral. This unfortunate incident revealed that a positive school climate had existed and now had even been strengthened significantly as people pulled together in a time of need.

When a school is characterized by *a positive school climate,* an observer might see, hear, or feel...

Visitors to the building receiving a warm reception.

—■—

A physical plant that is clean and well maintained.

—■—

The orderly and purposeful movement of students from place to place as they pursue learning activities.

57

Maintaining a positive climate

A positive middle school climate fosters students' interest in learning and becoming lifelong learners. Teachers who work in a positive environment feel good about themselves and their work, thereby creating a positive environment for their students. Vatterott (1991) in "Assessing School Climate in the Middle Level School," stated, "Improvement of school climate depends more on the behavior of adults than any other factor. Changing takes time and effort, but is possible if all adults work together toward a common goal" (p. 7). The Law of Positive Reinforcement states: "In the absence of positive reinforcement from appointed leaders, negative human attitudes and behaviors are most likely to emerge from the group being led" (De-Bruyn, 1996, p. 1). This truth makes it clear that the maintenance of a positive school climate is an ongoing process requiring almost daily reaffirmation.

Like young adolescents, the climate of a developmentally responsive middle level school requires constant nurturing.

To maintain a positive school climate with accompanying high staff morale requires attention in four areas: recognition, communication, shared leadership, and opportunities for growth. Specific ways to provide the recognition that will foster a positive climate are these.

- Certificates or notes placed in individual faculty boxes recognizing an accomplishment or expressing appreciation
- Providing refreshments at all meetings
- Including in the daily bulletin a "hats-off" note to share an individual's achievement
- A stand-up faculty meeting to celebrate accomplishments

Communication techniques that will nurture the positive school climate include

- Weekly staff newsletter, informative but professional
- Daily team meetings with clear expectations and an agenda
- The existence of a school-wide calendar that is regularly updated
- Ready access to telephone for all faculty and staff
- Regularly scheduled faculty meetings with an active agenda

The contribution of shared leadership to the maintenance of a positive school climate can be achieved in these ways.

- Faculty meetings run by staff
- Every faculty member is a part of at least one committee
- Scheduling is done by teachers with administrative support
- Staff development programs selected by and presented by teachers.

Finally, maintaining a positive school climate via the area of growth opportunities calls for such activities as these.

- Establishing a buddy system that would give teachers a colleague for honest sharing and communication
- Utilizing teachers with particular competencies in peer coaching arrangements
- Serving as cooperating teachers for pre-service teachers
- Encouraging the development of teacher portfolios
- Encouraging and supporting faculty as presenters at professional meetings and conferences.

Pitfalls to avoid

While it is certain that America's middle schools have improved in many areas during the past 25 years, they still have not reached the goal of providing an appropriate education to all adolescents. That is essentially the conclusion of the status study *America's Middle Schools: Practices and Programs – A 25 Year Perspective* (McEwin, Dickinson, & Jenkins, 1996).

—■—

Banners, posters, displays, and other indicators of pride in student accomplishments are visible.

—■—

The school's mission statement is prominently displayed.

— ▪ —

Volunteers, including parents and community members, are present and involved.

The weaknesses of middle school education should be acknowledged and frankly discussed and ... successes should be recognized and celebrated. Before significant long-term reform of middle level education can become a reality, we must indeed know where we are, how far we have come, where we should be headed, and how to get there. (p. 129).

Turning Points 2000: Educating Adolescents for the 21st Century (Jackson & Davis, 2000) reached a similar conclusion.

Although middle schools have continued to improve, it is clear that many thousands of young adolescents continue to attend middle schools where the programs and practices followed do not reflect what is known about exemplary middle level teaching, learning, and schooling and what has been advocated for many years.

For example, while the majority of middle level schools organize interdisciplinary teams, they rarely practice integrated curriculum but, instead, maintain highly departmentalized instruction. Furthermore, middle grades teachers still rely almost exclusively on direct instruction methods, such as lectures, and are less likely to use recommended strategies such as discussions, investigations, and cooperative learning groups. Although the majority of teachers who work with young adolescents have at least one planning period per day, research and experience indicate that they need at least two daily planning periods to enable them to work with team members in ways that increase achievement. In addition, in the majority of schools nationwide, the bulk of the faculty have received little specialized middle school professional training.

Johnston and Williamson (1996) stated the crisis we face in middle level education in these strong words.

Interactions among staff members and between students and staff reflect democracy and fairness.

Middle level education stands at a cross roads. As this century draws to a close, it can continue to march down the road of orthodoxy, expending its efforts on reproducing the characteristics of the "ideal" middle level school, or it can venture down a new road – one that focuses the middle level school on its rightful role: responsiveness to client needs. (p. 1).

The achievement of a positive school environment is almost a prerequisite for achieving any of the other reforms needed. A personalized school environment strengthens students' commitment to school, enhances their engagement in learning, and paves the way for faculty and staff to move the middle school beyond its organizational successes and tackle the difficult but critical matter of curriculum and instruction.

— ■ —

There exist feelings of warmth that visitors as well as regular attendees can feel, observe, and articulate.

In Summary

With increased student achievement as the ultimate goal, the establishment and maintenance of a positive school climate is a crucial means of achieving that goal. A school's administration and staff have the major responsibility for seeing that the right atmosphere exists to carry out the mission of the institution; it cannot be achieved without their contribution. The suggestions contained herein could serve as a starting point for dialogues to occur among both faculty and other stakeholders; Furthermore, attempts to separate climate and environmental issues from the academic mission are unlikely to lead to the desired results. ■

References

DeBruyn, R. L. (1996). Why administrative assistance and positive reinforcement are necessary on a weekly basis for teachers. *The MASTER Teacher*. Manhattan, KS: The Master Teacher, Inc.

Holland, H. (1996). Study shows middle schools have room to grow. *High Strides, 9* (1), 14-15.

Jackson, A., & Davis, G. (2000). *Turning points 2000: Educating adolescents in the 21st century.* New York: Teachers College Press.

Johnston, H. J., & Williamson, R. D. (1996). *Through the looking glass: The future of middle level education.* Reston, VA: National Association of Secondary School Principals.

McEwin, C. K., Dickinson, T. S., & Jenkins, D. M. (1996). *America's middle schools: Practices and programs—a 25 year perspective.* Columbus, OH: National Middle School Association.

Observations provided by Scott Conroy and Lisa Racine, Mount View Middle School, Marriottsville, Maryland. Scott and Lisa also contributed to the article.

National Middle School Association. (1995). *This we believe: Developmentally responsive middle level schools*. Columbus, OH: Author

Vatterott, C. (1991, April). Assessing school climate in the middle level school. *Schools in the middle: Theory into practice*. Reston, VA: National Association of Secondary School Principals.

Original article appeared in the November 1998 issue of *Middle School Journal, 30* (2), 65-67.

8. Curriculum That Is Challenging, Integrative, and Exploratory

Chris Stevenson

One sunny afternoon early in the fall of 1996, I left my office a bit early to catch the second half of a soccer game on campus. As I climbed into the sparsely filled grandstand, I noticed a row of seven or eight young adolescent girls and boys chattering among themselves while watching the game together. Not one to pass up such a good opportunity for a "double feature," I took a seat behind the middle of their row. This was an irresistible opportunity to unobtrusively check out a sample of adolescent culture while at the same time watching some soccer.

Their talk was wide ranging, jumping quickly from topic to topic. Sometimes they seemed to agree, but more often it was as if the conversation was competition for the most profound statements of fact and opinion. Unable to detect any coherent theme from the center of the row, I eased my way to one end where Joe was attempting to explain soccer rules to Amy, who was earnestly attentive. An apparent novice to the sport, she struggled to understand and to reassure him that his tutorial made sense to her. Try as he might, however, Joe's explanations of the offside rule in particular did not quite clean up Amy's confusion. Although she tried mightily, it was clear that she just was not getting it. He finally concluded his lesson with the reassurance that, "it makes a lot more sense when you're doing it."

I think Joe is onto something fundamentally important to our quest for middle level curriculum and pedagogy. He understands that knowledge derives from firsthand engagement of the subject matter – a widely espoused truth among middle level educators that is too infrequently the focus for adults' curriculum decisions. The most steadfast rationale for the middle school concept including widely diverse proposals concerning curriculum is a dogged emphasis on accommodating the "unique characteristics and needs of young adolescents." (National Middle

> In developmentally responsive middle level schools, curriculum embraces every planned aspect of a school's educational program. ...Although learning occurs in many unanticipated ways, curriculum is intentionally designed to accomplish a school's mission.

When the *curriculum is challenging, integrative, and exploratory,* an observer might see, hear, or feel...

— ■ —

Active classrooms with students working individually, in pairs, and/or in small groups.

— ■ —

A sense of community demonstrated through mutual respect and responsible behavior. Students and teachers sharing in the planning of curriculum and mutually engaged in addressing questions and concerns.

School Association, 1995, p. 20). Yet, our search for the composition of that curriculum seems inevitably reduced to discussions and proposals within "disciplines vs. interdisciplinary" or "subject specific vs. integrated" dualities. Interesting and often entertaining but irresolvable debates too easily divert us from our espoused goal of creating successful matches between our kids and their studies. The issue is not whether life is inherently discipline-based or interdisciplinary. I submit that Joe would have us seek and find our direction by examining more closely the interactions between the subject matter (e.g. soccer rules) and meaning (e.g. his and Amy's understanding). Authentic learning leaves unmistakable tracks in the talk and behavior of learners.

What should be the primary purpose of curriculum at the middle level? *This We Believe* (1995) posits that curriculum should be "challenging, integrated, and exploratory" (p. 20). It is fair to rejoin, "To whom?" Might such descriptors be used to justify any curriculum content or program or guide for any age students? If our focus is truly on young adolescent learners, then we will see to it that our emphasis is on *their* challenging and being challenged by their schoolwork, *their* successfully integrating new learnings into their continuously modified existing knowledge, and *their* exploring the ideas and questions that interest them.

We middle level educators must keep certain focus on the ways our students are growing and changing during these transition years between childhood and full adolescence. We know with certainty that they undergo distinctive changes from the ways of their earlier childhood. We also know that there is a great deal of variability among them; differentness is the norm in early adolescence. Mounting evidence indicates that individuals change according to idiosyncratic schedules, and they also develop uniquely in terms of intelligence, disposition, attitudes and tastes, interests, work habits, and aspirations. It seems to me that the abundance of possibilities for children during this brief period of human life invites curriculum initiatives that complement individual differences and transcend established curriculum paradigms. This perspective does not demean those curricula; rather, it ensures that our focus on the growth and development of individual children is preserved. For this brief period of schooling, our abiding concern must be the effectiveness with which our children learn both how to learn and the disposition that they can learn successfully.

What if our primary purpose in planning curriculum is to ensure the healthy development of young adolescent learners? What are their predominant needs as learners and citizens? Three decades of interviews with young adolescent students and countless collaborations as a middle level teacher point to some inherent needs that can be gratified through curriculum designs that preserve learner efficacy as the focal point. Students who demonstrate personal efficacy in school and in their relationships with peers and adults exhibit some essential traits.

Competence

Young adolescents care a great deal about being competent. Successful students identify themselves by the things they do well, and they relish opportunities to do those things. Whether it is running, or spelling, or shooting baskets, or solving equations, a powerful need for personal expertise perseveres. It does not follow that individuals have to be the very best at their particular competency, that no one else is equally as good as they are. But it does seem to matter that one be somewhat set apart from others by this expertise. The very best of circumstances is when classmates and significant others, especially older adolescents and adults, also acknowledge one's competence. Good curriculum from students' perspectives assures that they grow steadily in competencies that they acknowledge as useful and worthwhile. When youngsters are failing to grow in competence in their own eyes and in the perceptions of others, a fundamental developmental need is being denied.

—■—

Students passing on information about resources or newly learned computer skills through peer tutoring.

Responsibility

A second attribute of young adolescent learners who seem to be thriving is their perception of themselves as accountable and responsible in ways that approximate adulthood. They know they are not yet ready for a more fully independent adult role, but they value being able to take greater responsibility for themselves as well as being recognized for evidence of greater maturity. Initiative, dependability, and resourcefulness are qualities they value in themselves and each other. They care about being at ease with planning and organizing learning, working either alone or with selected peers. They prefer to think of themselves as good choosers and fair judges, and their personally constructed academic portfolios exude personal accountability and self-awareness. Curriculum that matches well with these qualities cultivates the very self-reliance we know to be essential to successful learners and strong individuals.

—■—

Through the work in progress it is clear students are forming values and making judgments, not just learning bits of information.

Affiliation

As a longtime teacher of young adolescents and observer of others who teach them well, I have noted that when curricu-

—■—

Students confidently presenting projects that reflect their pride of ownership and positive self-concepts.

lum is at its best it takes on something of a life of its own. There is a palpable "curriculum transcendence" through which students derive remarkable degrees of engagement and energy. Observe students preparing a drama production or doing a project together: they give lots of energy to such work, and in turn they are energized by it. Such experiences become benchmarks of future learning, and students articulate intense feelings of affiliation with those learning events. Sometimes the significance of the experience is wrapped up in values of momentous working relationships with peers as well as between them and adults, usually teachers, but often people outside the usual teaching staff such as parents or community members. At its very best, after all, learning is an energy loop: one invests energy in a process that in turn returns energy. Whatever curriculum unit middle level teachers may choose to teach, if there is no evidence of passion and ownership, enduring learning is not likely occurring.

— ■ —

Students arguing their point of view, persuading, laughing, talking, and debating.

Awareness

No one likes to be taken for a fool, especially young adolescents. Perhaps because of the intensity of the identity formation process, these youngsters are especially sensitive about how they are perceived and treated by others. Note their language, humor, dress, and interactions with peer groups as evidence of their need to be regarded by others as "with it." Being involved, savvy, and "tuned in" are paramount. Believing that "I know what's going on," affirms a sense of worth. Insights about one's abilities and strengths give rise to reflections and theories about how things are and how things should be done. I have found young adolescents to be especially responsive to inquiries designed to explain their perceptions about the dynamics of peer relationships, their school, and the community (Stevenson, 1998). Curriculum that serves these students well provides a climate and context in which they recognize the relevance of their studies and have ample

Curriculum is integrative when it helps students make sense out of their life experiences.

opportunities to demonstrate their knowledge to others, especially parents, older adolescents, and community people.

Ethical perception of self

Perhaps the most reassuring indicator of sound education and human development is evidence of our children's natural inclination toward moral ideals. How crucial it is for them to regard themselves as good people of high moral standing. Their growing interest in existential questions, concern about injustices, and readiness for activism in worthy causes signals the youngster's need to believe in himself or herself as a good person, an individual of worth who is making a difference in the world. Advocacy for animals, stewardship of the environment, and compassion for the needy and disadvantaged are natural causes they are eager to support as a matter of principle. As they grow in knowledge of the exigencies of political and economic systems, they come to recognize both the promise and vulnerabilities of democracy. A growing sophistication about how things work in a morally conscious and responsible community portends active citizenship that brings vitality to the school today and the larger community tomorrow. Any curriculum design that does not provide opportunities and support for student to do "right things" alongside the significant adults in their lives is sadly incomplete. Kids understand the value of being good through doing good.

David Hamburg (1993) has stated well the primary purpose and nature of middle level curriculum:

> What are the requirements for healthy adolescent development? In my view, it is essential that we help young adolescents to acquire constructive knowledge and skills, inquiring habits of mind, dependable human relationships, reliable basis for learning respect, a sense of belonging in a valued group, and a way of being useful to their communities. (p. 467)

Given the range of developmental diversity among children during these years, it does not seem possible for any single curriculum plan conceived by adults in isolation from a particular group of students and administered to all students at the same time to possibly accommodate everyone. Fortunately, such a single plan is not our only option. One of the great benefits of working with these students is their readiness to make responsible choices as to what they will study and learn. The more choices they are able to make, the more seriously they are in-

— ■ —

The excitement of discovery and the passion of investigating one's interests generates an energy that is electric.

Observations provided by Susan Boyer, Milton Middle School, Milton, Vermont.

67

clined to trust the choices adults are also making for them. Perhaps the greatest challenge to us as educators is to summon the courage to form partnerships with students by which we share curriculum planning. Beane's work (1993) compels us to enter into just such coalitions, and student-maintained records of their work in portfolios enables us to more fully understand the extent to which curriculum is actually cultivating competence and responsibility as well as testimonials of affiliation, awareness, and ethical perceptions of themselves.

Early in my teaching career I read in a now long-forgotten source that curriculum was urgently in need of major overhaul. The writer cautioned, however, that to throw out existing programs in favor of all new designs would bring about certain catastrophe. The essay went on to encourage that educators resolve to build 15% of their curriculum around the expressed needs and interests of their students. We were advised to treat that modest 15% as professional inquiry conceived to better understand the studies and pedagogy that best served our students. The remaining 85% of our curriculum could remain unchanged for the moment. The crucial advice was that we incorporate insights drawn from the 15% into the remaining 85%, and thereby remake subsequent curriculum in ways that will be more closely aligned with the particular characteristics and needs of our students. In so doing, we affirm ourselves as professionals who adapt practices according to insights resulting from our inquiries. Students like Amy and Joe will thank us. ■

References

Beane, J. A. (1993). *A middle school curriculum: From rhetoric to reality* (2nd ed.). Columbus, OH: National Middle School Association.

Hamburg, D. A. (1993). The opportunities of early adolescence. *Teachers College Record, 94* (3), 466-471

National Middle School Association. (1995) *This we believe: Developmentally responsive middle level schools*. Columbus, OH: Author.

Stevenson, C. (1998) *Teaching ten to fourteen year olds* (2nd ed.). White Plains, NY: Longman.

Original article appeared in the March 1998 issue of *Middle School Journal, 29* (4), 55-57.

9. Varied Teaching and Learning Approaches

Barbara L. Brodhagen

The section on "Varied Teaching and Learning Approaches" in National Middle School Association's *This We Believe* (1995) challenges all those connected with schools, but especially teachers, to work toward providing teaching and learning situations that invite and promote opportunities for maximum learning by every student. Very simply put, the document states that there is not a single best way to teach all children. If a teacher believes this and wants to maximize the possibility that every student does well, then the title of this section suggests the way to proceed: provide varied teaching and learning approaches. However, this belief statement must coexist with all of the other belief statements in the document, two of them in particular: "Curriculum that is challenging, integrative, and exploratory" and "assessment and evaluation that promote learning."

This chapter presents several strategies some teachers are using that seem to address a good deal of what is called for in the section on varied teaching and learning approaches. These will include using learning inventories, question posing by young adolescents, projects, and interactive and reflective learning by students. Finally some attention will be given to the need for professional development for teachers who are expected to use these approaches. In this commentary I write from my experience as a practicing classroom teacher as well as theory and research about teaching and learning approaches found in the literature.

Varied teaching and learning approaches connect the curriculum with assessment. These three must be present each day in every classroom. If curriculum is to be challenging, integrative, and exploratory then the teaching and learning practices selected must also be challenging, integrative, and exploratory. What exactly does this mean? This section of *This We Believe* correctly starts with a reminder that young adolescents have distinctive developmental and learning characteristics. As a

> The distinctive developmental and learning characteristics of young adolescents provide the foundation for selecting teaching strategies....Since young adolescents learn best through engagement and interaction, learning strategies feature activities that provide hands-on experiences and actively involve youngsters in learning.

69

When *varied teaching and learning approaches* are used, an observer might see, hear, or feel...

— ■ —

Decisions about content, use of time, assessment, and projects being made by teachers and students in collaboration.

— ■ —

Classrooms that are inviting and evidence purposeful work.

— ■ —

Student voice being honored, encouraged, and expected by all team members.

seventh grade teacher I can assure you that there are no two students alike in my classroom, even though all are approximately the same chronological age. What works for one might not necessarily work for the rest of the class. The knowledge, skills, and abilities they bring reflect the individuals they are, and it is up to us to find ways for each student to draw upon and demonstrate the strengths they already possess while learning new knowledge and skills.

Teachers who are serious about responding to the multiple intelligences and learning styles of their students make efforts to identify those learning styles. Some teachers use formal inventories or assessments to help discover students' strengths and talents. Other teachers have students complete a questionnaire that might include open-ended statements like the following:

- I learn best when I...
- In my spare time I really like to...
- I know when I really want to concentrate I have to...
- The best time for me to read is...
- When I think about making something with my hands I...

Still other teachers recognize that young adolescents have had a lot of experience in school and ask the students to tell how they believe they learn best. In addition to these three methods of gaining information about students' learning styles, it is a good idea to explain to them why and what we are doing. By explaining the idea of multiple learning styles, for example, students might be able to understand times when they have been unsuccessful in their learning and begin to articulate how other strategies might help them learn.

Many teachers know quite a bit about the different teaching strategies we are expected to and probably do use. For example, cooperative learning groups can be a powerful instructional strategy when used correctly. Direct teaching can be effective when used appropriately. Presenting information through both visual and auditory methods increases retention of material. The use of advanced organizers, anticipatory sets, or scaffolding helps students understand and remember more when new ideas or information are connected to prior learning. Connecting learning to real-life situations makes learning more meaningful and accessible. This list could become quite long. The next section addresses a few of these teaching and learning strategies that have particular promise.

Question Posing

"Varied Teaching and Learning Approaches" challenges educators to engage students in "diverse ways of posing and solving questions ... [building upon] the knowledge students already possess" (NMSA, 1995, p. 24). In order to do this, students need to have an opportunity to ask their own questions. These questions themselves might become the focus for the curriculum (Brodhagen, 1995; Beane, 1993), or young adolescents might be asked to raise questions for a teacher-selected theme, or they might even be given the opportunity to generate questions for a chapter's focus. In each of these approaches students would be asked to think about what they already know and help determine what else needs to be learned.

To help teachers do this, one might look at our Australian colleagues' attempts at "negotiating the curriculum" (Boomer, Lester, Onore, & Cook, 1994). They call for learner engagement, as seen when students become curious or puzzled about their learning; exploration as students take risks in their learning as they are challenged, yet supported; and reflection as students talk about what it is they have learned and experienced. These teachers help students identify and use the knowledge and skills they already possess. Four questions are presented to assist learners in focusing in on the problem, question, or issue of their intended study (United States teachers use a variation of this commonly referred to as "K-W-L").

1. What do we know already? (Or where are we now, and what don't we need to learn or be taught about?)
2. What do we want, and need, to find out? (Or what are our questions, what don't we know, and what are our problems, curiosities, and challenges?)
3. How will we go about finding out? (Where will we look, what experiments and inquiries will we make, what will we need, what information and resources are available, who will do what, and what should be the order of things?)
4. How will we know, and show, that we've found out when we've finished? (What are our findings? What have we learned? Whom will we show? For whom are we doing the work? and Where next? (p. 21)

Asking students to list or tell what it is they already know reinforces their view about self as a successful learner, builds upon prior learning, and begins to provide the linkage to new learning that will be integrated into existing personal knowledge and understandings. This is supported by past and emerg-

— ■ —

A multiage team operating, assuring long-term teacher-student relationships.

— ■ —

A class engaged in a weekly goal-setting session. Students outline the tasks to be completed in the thematic unit.

ing research in which positive effects have been reported in the areas of mathematics, science, the arts, language arts, and social studies (Cawelti, 1995).

When young adolescents are invited to participate in the planning of their own learning they do suggest varied learning activities. They name activities they like and those in which they do well. This includes activities that are visual, auditory, kinesthetic, interpersonal, mathematical, artistic, and so on. Drawing upon my own experience asking students to suggest activities to answer their questions within a particular theme (Brodhagen, 1995), I have learned young adolescents are quite skilled at naming a wide variety of activities that can be used to construct learning situations that build upon their learning strengths.

For example, a question raised in one of our student planned themes was, "Who am I?" Students' suggestions for activities that might be used to answer that question included: creating a life map that highlights events in their lives by either drawing pictures or using photos with captions explaining the event, interviewing a couple of their relatives to recall what the student was like earlier in her or his life, constructing a "trading card" highlighting important life statistics, and completing a family tree including ancestral background. In a different theme, "Outer Space: The Mysteries Above and Beyond," the question, "What is our solar system?" generated these suggestions: (a) make a model of our solar system in the classroom, (b) do a research project on all the parts of the solar system, (c) have a guest speaker, (d) visit the university Space Place, and (e) go to Kennedy Space Center. We were unable to do the last of these, but the point is that the students themselves were able to generate many ideas for varied learning activities.

— ■ —

All seventh grade classes organizing their portfolios in preparation for the upcoming student-led conferences. One class is engaged in mock conferences as a part of the preparation.

— ■ —

An informal team meeting before school starts to review the day's schedule that is to include an all-team activity.

Projects

If we have students raise questions about a unit, problem, issue, or theme to be studied, whether it was selected by the students or the teacher, and if we ask students to participate in naming or suggesting activities, then we will likely be considering the use of "projects." Project-based learning has been a part of the educational scene for most of this century (Kilpatrick, 1918). Projects are standard in most classrooms where curriculum integration or multidisciplinary curriculum approaches are used. Projects are authentically integrative; it would be difficult to imagine any project that did not utilize knowledge and skills from several disciplines.

According to Blumenfeld, Soloway, Marx, Krajcik, Guzdial, and Palincsar (1991, p. 370), there are two essential components of projects: "they require a question or problem that serves to organize and drive activities" and "these activities [must] result in a series of artifacts, or products, that culminate in a final product that addresses the driving question." The question itself can be determined by either the teacher or student, however,

> the students' freedom to generate artifacts is critical, because it is through this process of generation that students construct their knowledge; the doing and learning are inextricable. Artifacts are representations of the students' problem solutions that reflect emergent states of knowledge. (p. 372)

Here again we can see how students' individual learning styles and strengths would be accommodated by their involvement in the creation of the artifact. A project plan implicitly or explicitly requires students to state or reflect upon what it is they already know about the question or problem that is the focus of their project. The new information learned builds or is constructed upon students' existing knowledge. Using the four questions posed by Boomer and colleagues as suggested earlier can help achieve these ends.

Projects also provide students opportunities to use multiple resources including technology, popular culture, common "experts" (people in their personal community who know much about a topic), multicultural resources, and personal experiences. When students use diverse resources such as these, it is more likely they will be motivated to complete a project. It is when students create projects that we begin to see how they have made what they have learned meaningful and personal. Furthermore, in making project presentations students actually "perform knowledge" (Beane, 1997).

Projects can also accommodate individual differences among those young adolescents who might be labeled as having different kinds of educational needs, for example students labeled "learning disabled" or "emotionally disturbed." Since there is no one way to complete a project, each one can and probably will look different; and when they are evaluated, different looking projects could receive similar ratings. As a result, students with "special needs" have opportunities to demonstrate their knowledge using the skills they do have rather than simply failing because of those they do not have.

— ■ —

The team's yearly schedule identifies thematic units, the annual musical, end-of-the-year camping trip, along with school-wide tests, etc.

— ■ —

Students have varied opportunities to self-assess and reflect on the work they do: weekly goals assessments, portfolio organization, portfolio conferences, self-assessments on thematic unit goals and other learning activities.

Projects also provide opportunities for interaction among students as well as between students and teachers. This interaction can be instructional and evaluative, and it can even be considered social. Beane and Lipka (1984) reported three features of schooling in which students said they "felt good about themselves at school." They are "I get to work with my friends," "we have fun," and "the teacher is nice." What young adolescents were talking about is a teacher who lets kids work in pairs, cooperative groups, or as peer tutors; a teacher who has them "do" things, like projects, plays, media productions, and so on; and a teacher who treats them with respect, which includes giving them challenging work.

Finally, technology can be a useful tool in many student- or teacher-designed projects. Most students can gain access to more information when using technology. It allows them to get more up-to-date facts, for example weather and economic status reports; to correspond more quickly with other adolescents; and to access a wider range of data bases. And of course, using a word processor allows for corrections and revisions in a less labor intensive manner.

Fortunately, we now have many teacher accounts which include numerous examples of projects that we can go to for ideas and guidance. Some of these are *Integrated Studies in the Middle Grades: Dancing Through Walls* (Stevenson & Carr, 1993), *Dissolving Boundaries* (Brazee & Capelluti, 1995), *Beyond Separate Subjects: Integrative Learning at the Middle-Level* (Siu-Runyan & Faircloth, 1995), *Whole Learning in the Middle School: Evolution and Transition* (Pace, 1995), *Learning Through Real-World Problem Solving* (Nagel, 1996) and *Democratic Schools* (Apple & Beane, 1995).

Interactive Learning and Student Reflection

A growing number of teachers are finding that student learning is enhanced through interaction and reflection about what is being learned. In other words, having students talk about their learning can increase their understanding and mastery of new ideas. When we ask young adolescents to explain what it is they have read in literature, to talk through how they have solved a math problem, to draw a web, to explain their position on a social studies issue, or to discuss a final integrating project about an issue or problem, we are asking them to use critical thinking and processing skills, to synthesize content, and to make obvious their own meanings. This kind of interaction benefits both the speaker and the listener (Cawelti, 1995).

— ■ —

Students of varying abilities working side by side, sharing strengths and strengthening areas that challenge.

My teaching partners and I have arranged for interaction and reflection in many ways. Whole class discussions serve as a forum for students to explain learning processes and to hear strategies used by others. Partners or triad groups are used the same way. Journal writing and end-of-week "processing" sessions offer time for reflection about personal and whole-group learning experiences. We also suspect they improve at-home conversations when young adolescents actually have an answer to the question, "what are you doing in school?"

Like other teachers, we have also found that student-led parent conferences are a very powerful way of having students interact about and reflect on their learning. On these occasions, students explain to parents, guardians, or other significant adults what and how they have learned; how they have dealt with problems; how they have demonstrated their learning; and what goals they have set for further learning. These conferences are especially meaningful when they are a part of a comprehensive plan for students to self-evaluate their work.

Professional Development

There is much out there to help educators increase the likelihood of success for young adolescents. We have a wide research base to draw upon; and although each school context is different and individual study results might vary, enough work has been done to say that some teaching and learning strategies are better than others. This brings me to a final issue that needs to be addressed. Teachers, I believe, do want to do their very best. We want to be successful teachers who are teaching successful learners. We do want all children to learn. But, we cannot do this alone. Speaking for myself, I hear about new teaching and learning strategies and end up feeling guilty because I am not using them, yet I wonder when will I find the time to learn and prepare how to use them. It is easy to say "teachers should," but harder to find the time and ways to make this happen.

In schools genuinely responsive to young adolescents, the teachers and administrators also hold high expectations for themselves and for one another.

— ■ —

Together students and teachers identify diverse indicators of quality for a rubric that will be used to evaluate performance.

Observations provided by Carol Smith, Shelburne Middle School, Shelburne, Vermont.

School administrators, school boards, teacher unions, and the wider community must realize, as was reported in a recent report from the National Commission on Teaching and America's Future (1996), that good teachers are the most important element of successful learning. One of the best ways to improve student achievement is to continually improve the quality of the teaching staff. This means that teachers need to have adequate time to prepare to use teaching and learning strategies with which they might not be familiar. A one-hour inservice presentation is not enough for most teachers to implement a new teaching practice. Teachers need time to read research and decide whether a strategy can serve the needs of students. Teachers need opportunities to come together, for example in teacher or action research groups, to discuss what results or effects are seen as changes are implemented (Burnaford, Beane, & Brodhagen, 1994).

In my own district, groups of teachers are able to come together throughout the year to study their own practice, including teaching and learning strategies that promote the ideas of curriculum integration, as well as other questions they might want to study through action or teacher research. When teachers can actively study their own practice and its effects on students in their classroom, real change in teaching and learning strategies seems to occur. Furthermore, by doing action research teachers are better able to make informed decisions about which strategies should be continued.

These kinds of arrangements, regular workshops, visitation days, and adequate planning time, would go a long way toward providing the support needed to learn about and plan for the kinds of ideas included in *This We Believe*. If these were offered and used to move teachers over a long period of time, *This We Believe* might well become "This We Do." ■

References

Apple, M. W., & Beane, J. A. (1995). *Democratic schools.* Alexandria, VA: Association for Supervision and Curriculum Development.

Beane, J. A. (1993). *A middle school curriculum: From rhetoric to reality* (2nd ed.). Columbus, OH: National Middle School Association.

Beane, J. A. (1997*). Curriculum Integration: Designing the core of democratic education.* New York: Teachers College Press.

Beane, J. A., & Lipka, R. P. (1984). *Self-concept, self-esteem, and the curriculum.* Boston: Allyn and Bacon.

Blumenfeld, P., Soloway, E., Marx, R. W., Krajcik, J. S., Guzdial, M., & Palincsar, A. (1991). Motivating project based learning: Sustaining the doing, supporting the learning. *Educational Psychologist, 26* (3&4), 369-398.

Boomer, G., Lester, N., Onore, C., & Cook, J. (1994*). Negotiating the curriculum: Educating for the 21st century.* London: Falmer.

Brazee, E. N., & Capelluti, J. (1995*). Dissolving boundaries: Toward an integrative curriculum.* Columbus, OH: National Middle School Association.

Brodhagen, B. L. (1995). The situation made us special. In M. W. Apple & J. A. Beane (Eds.), *Democratic Schools.* (pp. 83-100). Alexandria, VA: Association for Supervision and Curriculum Development.

Burnaford, G., Beane, J., & Brodhagen, B. (1994). Teacher action research: Inside an integrative curriculum. *Middle School Journal, 26* (2), 5-13.

Cawelti, G. (Ed.). (1995). *Handbook of research on improving student achievement.* Arlington, VA: Educational Research Service.

Kilpatrick, W. H. (1918). The project method. *Teachers College Record, 19,* 319-335.

Nagel, N. G. (1996). *Learning through real-world problem solving.* Thousand Oaks, CA: Corwin.

National Commission on Teaching and America's Future. (1996). *What matters most: Teaching for America's future.* New York: Carnegie Corporation.

National Middle School Association. (1995). *This we believe: Developmentally responsive middle level schools.* Columbus, OH: author.

Pace, G. (Ed.). (1995). *Whole learning in the middle school: Evolution and transition.* Norwood, MA: Christopher-Gordon.

Siu-Runyan, Y., & Faircloth, C. V. (Eds.). (1995). *Beyond separate subjects: Integrative learning at the middle level.* Norwood, MA: Christopher-Gordon.

Stevenson, C., & Carr, J. E. (Eds.). (1993). *Integrated studies in the middle grades: Dancing through walls.* New York: Teachers College Press.

Original article appeared in the January 1998 issue of *Middle School Journal, 29* (3), 49-52.

10. Assessment and Evaluation that Promote Learning

Gordon F. Vars

Continuous, authentic, and appropriate assessment and evaluation are essential components of the learning process at any age level, providing information that students, teachers, and family members need to plan further learning.

In *This We Believe* the National Middle School Association (1995) urges educators to shift their focus from merely measuring and judging student progress to using assessment and evaluation to actively promote learning. Unfortunately, many current practices in schools at all levels actually impede learning, and middle level schools are no exception. Conventional competitive assessment, evaluation, and marking too often turn students into "grade junkies," who demand ABC marks or "points" for everything they do. Popular incentive programs in which students win prizes just for showing up in school further aggravate the "pay me" attitude that permeates our contemporary culture. Kohn (1993) has convincingly documented the pernicious effects of these and other "bribes," arguing that they are external means of controlling the behavior of other people, especially the young.

In contrast, NMSA's position paper advocates practices that foster student self-control and acceptance of responsibility for one's own actions. It is this kind of character and integrity, plus an inner-directed lifelong thirst for learning, that young people must have to become fully-functioning citizens in our democratic society. Self-motivated students will learn, not only basic knowledge and skills, but also the critical thinking skills and habits of mind required to deal with our rapidly changing world.

To accomplish this, the position paper states: "Middle level students need to participate in all phases of assessment and evaluation, helping to set individual and group goals, identifying ways to measure progress, and evaluating their own accomplishments" (National Middle School Association, 1995, pp. 26-27). This approach would appear to be contrary to the current emphasis on externally-imposed standards and assessment.

Going against the flow

Most of America's teachers today are anxious, if not paranoid, about preparing their students for state proficiency exams and other externally imposed assessments. Legislators, school board members, administrators, parents, and the general public are calling for "world-class" standards and demanding higher test scores at the very time when financial aid for public education is declining. Accountability, always present in any public service, has indeed turned into a nightmare for school people.

Under these circumstances, it may seem naïve to ask teachers to relinquish some of their power by making students full partners in the teaching-learning process. However, sharing does not mean abdication of responsibility, as exemplified by the name given to this approach years ago: teacher-student planning. The hyphen symbolizes cooperation and the teacher is named first to denote ultimate responsibility.

This approach was pioneered in the early days of this century (Giles, 1941; Miel & Associates, 1952), and has since been affirmed by research in human motivation and the importance of "locus of control." People with an external locus of control see their lives as controlled by other people or by "luck." They are unlikely to exert much effort on their own behalf, whether it be in preparing for an examination or carrying out tasks later as a member of the work force. On the other hand, people with an internal locus of control see themselves as having at least some influence over events. They are more likely to rise to whatever challenges face them, even earning a decent score on a state examination if they see benefits of that effort.

Hence it is important to invite students to work with their teachers to make critical decisions at all stages of the learning enterprise, especially goal-setting, establishing evaluation criteria, demonstrating learning, self-evaluation, peer evaluation, and reporting.

Goal setting

"Students should set personal standards and assess their progress in achieving both the knowledge and behavioral goals of an education" (National Middle School Association, 1995, p. 26).

Involving students in goal setting should begin on the very first day of class as students and teachers get acquainted and share their hopes for the coming year. Some middle school teachers start the year by challenging students with the question, "Why are you in school?" (Van Til, Vars, & Lounsbury,

When *assessment and evaluation promote learning,* an observer might see, hear, or feel...

— ■ —

Visual evidence of myriad opportunities for all students to express and exhibit their achievements in various media and formats is present.

— ■ —

Little emphasis on letter or numerical grades is evident. Instead, constructive comments from teachers and peers is found on student work. These comments include acknowledgment of successes and specific suggestions for ways to improve the product.

1961; Pate, Homestead, & McGinnis, 1997). After dealing with the typical young adolescent "flip" answers, teacher and students discuss why schooling is compulsory. This leads to a review of the knowledge, skills, and attitudes considered essential for effective citizenship. The class also may consider what it means to be a "good student." Such discussions provide a solid basis for the establishment of both personal and class goals for the year.

The beginning of the year also is the time to list the specific content and skills prescribed in both district and state standards for the grade level and subject. And students need to be informed about the exit standards they must meet in order in graduate from high school and the nature of any proficiency tests that lie ahead. Ideally, these "must learns" are posted in the classroom for reference all year as needed.

> —■—
>
> Narrative progress forms, designed with student input and including mechanisms for student self-assessment, teacher assessment, and parental responses are being reviewed with students.

At the same time students should be engaged in identifying issues, problems, and concerns, both personal and societal, that they believe merit study. Beane (1993, 1997) and Brodhagen (1995) are present-day champions of this approach to developing integrative curriculum, but the progressive educators who pioneered this kind of teacher-student planning applied it in all subjects (Aikin, 1942; Lipka et al., 1998).

With mandates on the table and major areas of student concern identified, teachers and students can then begin cooperatively establishing both personal and class goals. This phase of teacher-student planning lays the foundation for developing both a "curriculum that is challenging, integrative, and exploratory" and the "varied teaching and learning approaches" (National Middle School Association, 1995, pp. 20, 24) needed to carry it out. The challenge in any course is to identify themes or topics for study that are both relevant to students and also enable them to master mandated content and skills.

It is much more honest for teachers to present mandates "up front" and invite students to help plan how to meet them, rather than to inject them into thematic units presumably planned around student concerns. Hicks (1995) described how a mandated unit on the State of Maine was later inserted into the sequence of thematic units planned by a team with a class of mixed sixth, seventh, and eighth graders. The teachers also made sure that they taught the skills prescribed in Maine's Common Core of Learning.

Of course, teachers must have the final say, and there may well be some mandated content or skill that cannot be integrated into a unit meaningful to most students. If most decisions are made jointly, students usually will be good sports about studying this "extraneous" material, if only to help teachers out! Since few classes accomplish everything they set out to do in any one year, unit sequences need to be planned carefully to ensure that critical learning experiences are provided before time runs out.

In any case, goal setting should take into account both the interests and concerns of students and the expectations of society. The greater the student participation in this process, the greater will be their motivation for learning.

Establishing evaluation criteria

"Criteria for evaluation should be specified in advance and formulated with appropriate involvement of students and their parents or guardians." (National Middle School Association, 1995, p. 26). Cooperative planning of goals and objectives leads naturally to joint decisions on how progress will be assessed and what criteria will be applied. *This We Believe* calls for assessment that is "continuous, authentic, and appropriate" (p. 26). Assessment and evaluation are exceedingly complex processes, as tellingly illustrated in the ASCD Yearbook *Communicating Student Learning* (1996). Guskey (1996) reminded us in the yearbook that comprehensive assessment includes at least three components: product, process, and progress. Each of these requires different assessment procedures. Moreover, in every case a decision must be made as to "frame of reference" or basis of comparison: so-called absolute standards, norms based on performance of other students, or individual ability or progress.

Teachers today are making more and more use of performance assessment. While global assessments sometimes may be appropriate, most experts recommend establishing specific performance criteria. These criteria, often called rubrics, spell out in some detail what various levels of performance look like. Too often, however, these levels are translated directly to ABC marks, which further complicates the marking and grading issue that will be addressed later.

Considering the complexity of defining criteria or rubrics, it may seem overly optimistic to expect much participation of middle level students. The key word here, of course, is "appropriate." While fifth or sixth graders might be invited to suggest some general guidelines for judging student progress toward a goal, eighth or ninth graders, after several years' experience helping to design rubrics, probably could devise criteria that would meet with nearly any teacher's approval. Likewise, appropriate participation from some busy parents or guardians

— ■ —

A class engaged in peer assessments of works in progress.

— ■ —

On examining a student's portfolio, there is evidence that the student has edited, improved, and resubmitted works in order to perfect them.

might consist merely of signing a form that indicates they have read the proposed criteria and approve of them (Pate, Homestead, & McGinnis, 1997). In other situations, parents, students, and teachers might meet in small groups to brainstorm possibilities.

Willis (1996) described this process as carried out by Larry Lewin, who teaches eighth grade at James Monroe Middle School in Eugene, Oregon. Lewin invited his students to help generate criteria against which to assess the persuasive letter they wrote after a study of historic events in and around the year 1492. Students wrote to Ferdinand and Isabella of Spain, defining the encounter between Europeans and Native Americans as either a "discovery," a "visit," or an "invasion" and defending their points if view. Lewin affirms the importance of using class-generated assessment criteria so that students feel more ownership in the process.

Yet even experts on educational measurement continue to wrestle with how to make performance assessment valid and reliable, not to mention "honest" and "fair" (Wiggins, 1996). Teachers must not expect students to achieve absolute precision in defining levels of performance. And assessing a product like the persuasive letter that Lewin assigned should be balanced with other assessments of both process criteria and progress criteria. Hence *This We Believe's* call for using "a variety of assessment procedures" (p. 27). Over-reliance on performance assessment can be just as harmful as using only paper-and-pencil, multiple-choice tests, and then basing grades on class averages.

Demonstrating learning

"Students can assemble portfolios and carry out demonstrations that reveal growth in many dimensions and categories" (National Middle School Association, 1995, p. 27).

Teachers have long used individual or group presentations and reports for both teaching and assessment. Even with clear-cut criteria specified in advance, assessing these "exhibitions" may be problematical because of the "showmanship factor." Some self-assured and creative students may hide a shallow grasp of a topic with a "glitzy" presentation designed more to entertain than to inform. Both teachers and students must be encouraged to look for the real "meat" of student presentations.

Portfolios, as a way to organize and house evidence of student accomplishments, have many advantages (Lustig, 1996). However once again, teachers, students, and parents must beware of the showmanship factor and probe for evidence of genu-

—■—

A second round of student-led conferences reveals that students have improved the skills involved in planning and carrying out such conferences.

—■—

Visual and audible examples of students offering and accepting constructive criticism, suggestions for improvement, and recognition on a regular basis are noted.

ine understanding and skill. Students employ many higher-level thinking skills in selecting, explaining, and reflecting on their choices of what to include in a portfolio. This experience may, in the long run, prove to be more beneficial than any specific task documented in the portfolio.

It is clear that there are many difficulties in designing developmentally appropriate and technically sound assessment procedures. Nevertheless, students need to be involved as much as possible. Both teachers and students need to define carefully what they hope to accomplish and to talk with each other about these important matters.

Student self-evaluation

"Student self-evaluation is an important means of developing a fair and realistic self-concept" (National Middle School Association, 1995, p. 27).

Middle level students are at a crucial stage in the formation of wholesome self-concepts, so all school practices and procedures should be examined in this light. Engaging in self-evaluation and then sharing those insights with trusted and caring teachers and peers may help reduce the isolation, hopelessness, and despair that drive some young people to drugs, premature sex, and other harmful practices. Care must be taken, however, to avoid the artificial "make-em-feel-good" approaches sometimes marketed to enhance self-concept in hopes that it will increase academic achievement (Baumeister, 1996).

On the other hand, our culture sometimes makes it difficult for a person to express genuine pride in accomplishments for fear of being criticized for "bragging" or "apple-polishing." The goal is to give credit where credit is due and to help young people appreciate both their own and others' genuine accomplishments. If teachers and students are engaged in learning experiences that they both consider meaningful, honest but tactful assessment and evaluation will seem both appropriate and necessary. Pate, Homestead, & McGinnis (1997) demonstrated with numerous examples the critical role of self-reflection by both students and teachers in teacher-student-planned integrated curriculum.

Peer evaluation

"Occasional use of peer evaluation further demonstrates that teachers and students alike are involved in the assessment process" (National Middle School Association, 1995, pp. 27-28).

Young adolescents are judging one another much of the time, too often in terms of clothes or other material possessions

—■—

In small groups students are discussing quality issues.

—■—

In examining student journals it is apparent that students reflect on their goals, strategies to meet them, ways to determine when and how well a goal has been met, revisions of goals, and new strategies to improve in the future.

rather than character or accomplishments. In a classroom where trust has been established, this interest in peers can be converted from put-downs into thoughtful and helpful comments and suggestions. Of course, the assessment criteria should be clear, which they are likely to be if students and teachers jointly develop them. As students are learning to give positive feedback, peer-to-peer evaluations probably should be in writing and should be scanned by the teacher before delivery in order to screen out potentially hurtful comments.

— ■ —
Students are observed discussing and agreeing on goals.

Reporting

"Assessment and evaluation should emphasize individual progress rather than comparison with other students" (National Middle School Association, 1995, p. 27).

"Emphasis should be on what the student has accomplished, not the failure to reach some arbitrary uniform standard" (National Middle School Association, 1995, p. 28).

"Student-led conferences with teachers and family members are highly desirable and lead to continuous two-way communication between home and school" (National Middle School Association, 1995, p. 28).

The issues surrounding marking and reporting are complex and often controversial. In these three statements, *This We Believe* reaffirms the commitment to meeting the needs of individual young adolescents and takes a stand in opposition to many common practices in schools today. Most schools at all levels still use grades that compare student performance with class averages. Moreover, grades often include other factors, such as effort, progress, and even classroom behavior. Truly, most grades are a "witches brew" and no one really knows what is in them! In middle schools, which are intended to be responsive to the nature and needs of young adolescents, marking and reporting practices often undermine the staff's attempt to make education developmentally appropriate and humane. Indeed, competitive ABC marking directly violates three major needs and characteristics of middle level youth (Vars, 1992).

The first step is to "disaggregate" the information packed into the typical grade (Wiggins, 1996). Many schools already disaggregate to a limited extent, rating student effort and classroom behavior on different sections of the report card. This presumably makes the grade solely an indication of academic achievement.

But the question remains, "Achievement compared to what: the class average? grade level standards? individual progress? teacher expectations? In arguing for individualized assessment and evaluation, *This We Believe* forthrightly affirms that the emphasis should be on the individual. Distinctly different forms and procedures are needed to report different types of assessment, such as: where a student stands with reference to standards, the degree to which he or she meets reasonable expectations, and whether the student is making appropriate use of ability. Students and their parents are entitled to other information, too, such as rank in class on certain criteria, performance on normed national or state examinations, and even teacher or peer evaluations of classroom behavior. But all these evaluations must be reported separately, not combined, and primary emphasis should be on individual progress.

Lake and Kafka (1996) described a multifaceted reporting system used at Grand Avenue Middle School in Milwaukee, Wisconsin, that takes the place of traditional grades. Teachers at Harmon Middle School in Aurora, Ohio, also have made a major move in that direction. Report cards in this school carry as many as five different kinds of information, each presented in a different format.

Listed first on the report card is the teacher's rating of the student's "Personal-Social Development" in terms of "Work Habits" and "Behavior." These are marked

(O) Outstanding progress, (S) Satisfactory progress, and *(N) Needs improvement.* "Work Habits" may be further subdivided into eight specific criteria, such as *Brings material* or *Completes assignments.* Likewise, seven criteria may be listed under "Behavior," such as *Punctual* or *Respectful of Others.*

Next on the report is the teacher's estimate of each student's effort. This is stated in terms of how that individual's achievement compares with his or her "capacity." Three ratings are possible, ranging from "Working at or near capacity" to "Substantially below capacity."

The third section of the Harmon report card is a listing of critical pupil performance objectives for that subject and grade level, based on appropriate state guidelines. Each is marked as follows: *(C) Indicates competency at this time, (L) Lacks competency,* or *(N) Not assessed this grading period.* Each student also receives a letter grade for achievement, either ABCDF or OSN, and many report forms also include space for teacher comments.

With each teacher assessing up to 15 performance objectives annually, completing report cards every nine weeks, and sending progress reports midway through each grading period, the Harmon teachers spend a great deal of time on assessment.

— ■ —

Prominently posted in classrooms is evidence of students' personal goals, class aspirations, and curricular objectives, together with the rubrics designed to describe degrees of attainment for various educational ends.

Responsible middle level educators design assessment and evaluation activities that allow young men and young women equal opportunity when measuring academic progress.

They do this in order to communicate as accurately as possible with both students and parents.

If schools are to be held accountable for student learning, teachers must be given the time, not only to teach but also to assess student progress. As Wiggins (1996) reminds us, when thoughtful student assessment and evaluation are given the priority they deserve, schools will arrange schedules and teaching loads accordingly. Student involvement in the process relieves the burden somewhat, but teachers still bear ultimate responsibility.

Computers already provide some help. Too often, however, computer-based grading systems may make it easier and faster for teachers to do what they should not be doing at all — that is, converting complex human behavior into numbers to be crunched. Assessment experts also decry such common practices as averaging unlike data or factoring in prior student performance instead of looking only at what the student can do now (Guskey, 1996; Wiggins, 1996).

Brewer and Kallick (1996) described how technological innovations like digital portfolios and video progress reports may help to reduce time demands. But only a real live person can take into account the many factors that must be considered in making evaluations that are both honest and fair. Hence the *This We Believe* emphasis on portfolios and conferences.

The issue of success and failure is especially prominent in current discussion of standards. Standards set at "world-class levels," as some advocate, will virtually guarantee that many students will fail. Indeed, an influential report from the American Federation of Teachers (1996) calls for "absolute mastery," which few human beings can hope to achieve. Later the report does suggest the establishment of multiple levels of performance: "partially proficient," "proficient," and "advanced."

Even when the criteria for each level are carefully specified, it will be up to teachers to judge whether a student is proficient enough to be promoted to the next grade level. As always, the teacher's professional judgment is the key factor.

The threat of failure is especially harmful to vulnerable young adolescents. Years ago, Popper (1967) argued that one important function of the junior high or middle school is "protective intervention." By that he meant that students going through the sometimes traumatic changes associated with puberty should be protected from some of the outside pressures that permeate adult society. Imposition of arbitrary standards would clearly be one of those pressures he would urge us to delay as long as possible. As suggested earlier, making standards known to students and involving them in devising ways to measure and to achieve them should make the standards seem less threatening to impressionable young adolescents.

A parent-student-teacher conference, student-led or otherwise, ideally is the culmination of a long series of assessments and evaluations, all of them guided by crucial all-school policies like those discussed above. Giving students a leadership role in conferences is a vivid demonstration that school assessment and evaluation are primarily for the benefit of students. Through sharing and interpreting a portfolio with various kinds of evidence, a student further reinforces the notion that he or she is in charge of the learning process. Of course, conferences are but one of the many kinds of two-way communication between home and school needed to give students the support and encouragement they need.

Conclusion

Schools today have a dual obligation: to help students deal with personal and world concerns and at the same time meet standards and do well on externally-imposed examinations. The NMSA position paper argues that the best way to do this is to involve students directly in every step of the teaching-learning process. Assessment should emphasize individual progress, and varied reporting forms and procedures must be used, in keeping with the complexity of the human behavior being evaluated. The "bottom line" is not just grades or test scores but the development of decent, responsible, ever-learning young people.

In all deliberations in this complex aspect of education, educators should be guided by this statement from *This We Believe* that reflects the heart of middle level philosophy: "In developmentally responsive middle level schools, assessment

— ■ —

An impromptu celebration of the accomplishments of several students is witnessed in a total team gathering.

Observations provided by Mark Springer, Radnor Middle School, Wayne, Pennsylvania.

and evaluation procedures reflect the characteristics and uniqueness of young adolescents" (National Middle School Association, 1995, p. 27). ■

References

Aikin, W. (1942). *The story of the Eight-Year Study*. New York: Harper and Brothers.

American Federation of Teachers. (1996). A system of high standards: What we mean and why we need it. *American Educator, 20* (1), 22-27.

Association for Supervision and Curriculum Development. (1996*)*. *Communicating student learning* (1996 Yearbook). Alexandria, VA: Author.

Baumeister, R. E. (1996). Should schools try to boost self-esteem? *American Educator, 20* (2), 14-19, 43.

Beane, J. A. (1993). *A middle school curriculum: From rhetoric to reality* (2nd ed.). Columbus, OH: National Middle School Association.

Beane, J.A. (1997). *Curriculum integration: Designing the core of democratic education*. New York: Teachers College Press.

Brewer, W. R., & Kallick, B. (1996). Technology's promise for reporting student learning. In Association for Supervision and Curriculum Development, *Communicating student learning* (pp. 178-187). Alexandria, VA: Author.

Brodhagen, B. L. (1995). The situation made us special. In M. W. Apple & J. A. Beane (Eds.), *Democratic schools* (pp. 83-100). Alexandria, VA: Association for Supervision and Curriculum Development.

Giles, H. H. (1941). *Teacher-pupil planning*. New York: Harper.

Guskey, T. R. (1996). Reporting on student learning: Lessons from the past—prescriptions for the future. In Association for Supervision and Curriculum Development, *Communicating student learning* (pp. 13-24). Alexandria, VA: Author.

Hicks, B. G. (1995*)*. *Integrative units as middle level curriculum: An evaluative case study*. (Doctoral Dissertation, University of Maine). *Dissertation Abstracts International, 56* (10), A3826

Kohn, A. (1993). *Punished by rewards: The trouble with gold stars, incentive plans, A's, praise, and other bribes*. Boston: Houghton Mifflin.

Lake, J., & Kafka, K. (1996). Reporting methods in grades K-8. In Association for Supervision and Curriculum Development, *Communicating student learning* (pp. 114-115). Alexandria, VA: Author.

Lipka, R. P., Lounsbury, J. H., Toepfer, Jr., C. F., Vars, G. F., Alessi, Jr., S. P. , & Kridel, C. (1998). *The Eight-Year Study revisited: Lessons from the past for the present*. Columbus, OH: National Middle School Association.

Lustig, K. (1996*)*. *Portfolio assessment: A handbook for middle level teachers*. Columbus, OH: National Middle School Association.

Miel, A., & Associates. (1952). *Cooperative procedures in learning.* New York: Bureau of Publications, Teachers College, Columbia University.

National Middle school Association. (1995). *This we believe: Developmentally responsive middle level schools.* Columbus, OH: Author.

Pate, P. E., Homestead, E. R., & McGinnis, K. L. (1997*). Making integrated curriculum work: Teachers, students and the quest for coherent curriculum.* New York: Teachers College Press.

Popper, S. H. (1967). *The American middle school: An organizational analysis.* Waltham, MA: Blaisdell.

Van Til, W., Vars, G. F., & Lounsbury, J. H. (1961). *Modern education for the junior high school years.* Indianapolis, IN: Bobbs-Merrill.

Vars, G. F. (1992). Humanizing student evaluation and reporting. In J. L. Irvin (Ed.). *Transforming middle level education* (pp. 336-365). Boston: Allyn & Bacon.

Wiggins, G. (1996). Honesty and fairness: Toward better grading and reporting. In Association for Supervision and Curriculum Development, *Communicating student learning* (pp. 141-177). Alexandria, VA: Author.

Willis, S. (1996). On the cutting edge of assessment: Testing what students can do with knowledge. *Education Update (ASCD), 38* (4), 1, 4-7.

Original article appeared in the March 1997 issue of *Middle School Journal, 28* (4), 44-49.

11. Flexible Organizational Structures

Deborah Kasak

> Developmentally appropriate middle level schools are flexible in grouping, scheduling, and staffing. ...Teachers design and operate much of the program, collaborate across teaching specialties, and share responsibility for literacy development, guidance/ advocacy, and student life.

The operative word for middle level education has long been *flexibility.* Young adolescent needs and characteristics defy rigidity, and good schools for young adolescents are places that design their practice to reflect an understanding of young adolescent growth and development. *This We Believe* speaks to flexibility in grouping, scheduling, and staffing. Flexible structuring helps to create a responsive environment – in which needs can be recognized and adjustments made in form and function when necessary in order to maximize results. The best middle level schools are ever-changing, learning organizations.

The hallmark of an effective middle level school rests in its capacity to create dynamic learning teams within the school. Schools are organized into learning communities where close relationships between students and adults can be established and where more individualized attention can be given to all learners. Team structure alters and personalizes the working relationships between students and teachers, therefore enhancing the context wherein good instruction can thrive.

Over the last three decades of middle school implementation, schools and teams have experimented with many variations of interdisciplinary team organization. Teams, it is believed, contributed to greater student contact and increased personalization. Teams establish shared responsibility for student learning that reduces the stress of isolation among students and teachers. Finally, teams are the platform for creating greater coordination, collaboration, and integration of learning opportunities (Alexander & George, 1981; Arhar, Johnston, & Markle, 1988, 1989; Carnegie Council on Adolescent Development, 1989; Erb & Doda, 1989; George & Alexander, 1993; George & Oldaker, 1985; Gruhn & Douglass, 1947; Johnston, Markle, & Arhar, 1988). Full and vigorous implementation is the expectation and yet the level of implementation is a school-by-school situation and can be bound by the constraints of local fiscal and human resources. If interdisciplinary teams (one manifestation of flexible organizational structures) are advantageous, how do schools implement teams in a way that creates high performance learning communities for their students?

Team Tasks and Needs

When first considering flexible organizational structures for the entire school, staff members need to know what constitutes an effective team and what are adequate levels of resources a team must have in order to have a reasonable chance at improving academic outcomes for students. Answers to these questions determine school success.

The tasks and responsibilities of teams are many. Teams in their early stages of implementation focus on coordinating classwork, tests, student behaviors, parental contacts, and special team activities. Experienced teams progressively take on tasks that integrate curriculum, experiment with blocks of time, develop service learning projects, hold individual student conferences, or plan strategies to increase parental involvement. During common planning time, teams are most likely to engage in four broad sets of tasks: (a) curriculum coordination; (b) coordination of student assignments, assessments, and feedback; (c) parental contact and involvement; and (d) contact with other building resource staff. Each of the four broad areas of team function is composed of different activities. The depth of team functioning is progressive. Teams cannot do everything all at once, but as teams mature in their development, it is expected that they will perform the multitude of tasks with greater ease and more frequency. "Good functioning" teams cannot accomplish their objectives, tasks, and goals without sufficient time to plan and reasonable conditions within which to operate.

The presence of certain structural resources for teams makes their effectiveness more likely and supports their contribution to the overall developmental responsiveness of a school. Information first released in 1997 from a longitudinal study of reforming middle level schools in Illinois identifies several necessary conditions for modifying instruction to improve student achievement (Erb & Stevenson, 1999; Felner, et al., 1997; Flowers, Mertens, & Mulhall, 1999, 2000).

When *flexible organizational structures* are in place, an observer might see, hear, or feel...

— ■ —

A look at the master schedule indicates that except for lunch and exploratories, teams have complete control over how they use time.

— ■ —

The team leaders are to meet after school to decide how best to adjust schedules to accommodate the History Fair.

— ■ —

The principal's advisory council agenda includes two items: (1) whether to have individual ethnic celebrations or one large multicultural festival; (2) the request of two sixth grade partner teams to move with their groups to the seventh grade.

These studies have identified "threshold" resources needed for team effectiveness.

1. **Common planning time in excess of four times per week for an equivalent of 40 or more minutes per day.** This common planning time is in addition to a teacher's individual preparation period. To successfully influence instruction and improve student performance, teams of teachers need sufficient time for team "work" and the accomplishment of team tasks.

2. **Team sizes of under 120 students with smaller teacher/ student ratios.** Small communities for learning must be just that – small. Teacher teams of two, three, and four members effect more positive outcomes for students. Homeroom class sizes on the smaller teams of 25 students or fewer increase results and overall team performance.

3. **The length of time a team has been together.** Stable team composition contributes to productivity since teams learn how to improve their performance and functioning as they improve their teaming practices. Higher order team operations occur when teams move beyond the beginning stages of learning to work together. Stable teams make discussions about instruction and assessment a major activity for team planning.

If teams are given these structural resources with which to work, the likelihood of the team improving instruction and achievement is vastly strengthened. If teams are expected to function with less than these threshold resources then their impact is less promising. When schools are implementing flexible organizational structures, they need to adhere to at least these minimum levels of team resource needs.

These are necessary conditions, however, but in and of themselves not sufficient. This means that there are schools that provide teams with adequate common planning time, desirable team size, and longevity but do not attain high levels of performance. Flexible organizational structures provide the opportunity for high performance to flourish; however, the structural resources must be matched with high doses of determination, vision, will, and creativity to make teams perform well. To be successful, a school community keeps its vision of exemplary middle level education clearly focused, examines all of its practices to align them with its vision, and holds each and every student and teacher accountable for the attainment of its vision.

When implementing flexible structuring, the key is that teams need time to collaborate and work on instructional goals; for without these structural resources, they have less of a shot at achieving positive effects. Of course, there are schools that implement flexible organizational structures with less than these necessary conditions. Such schools may even report improvements in coordination and may feel more effective, but their range of impact is severely limited. Since schools and districts seek to implement middle level reform for the maximum benefits they can derive from this flexible organizational structure, they need to provide sufficient structural resources for teams to accomplish the task of improving student outcomes.

Applying Team Tasks and Needs to Responsive School Structures

When a school adopts the interdisciplinary team structure, it does so with several basics in mind. In its simplest form, a team is a common set of teachers who work with a common group of students in a common section of a building with common expectations and who have a separate, common team planning time. Interdisciplinary teams rely on adjusting the schedule for instructional goals which is made possible by the working relationship among the adults responsible for the academic progress of "common group of students" (see Seed, 1998).

To establish teams in schools both large and small, the strengths of the teaching staff need to be assessed and considered. Many schools have teachers prioritize their strengths and liabilities, do inventories or learning styles ratings, and ask for confidential feedback as to who they could effectively work with on a team. These assessments are used to form teams. Diversity within a teaching team is valued because of the wide array of tasks a team must perform in order to be effective. A good team presents a balanced lineup with good role players held together by their common commitment to the education of their students.

The size of teams is not static from grade-to-grade or year-to-year. On average, teacher team sizes range from two to five members. It is common for schools to begin with larger team sizes because teachers are more comfortable viewing team mem-

In lieu of academic tracking, schools use enrichment programs, cooperative learning groups, and independent study to respond to the variety of student competencies, interests, and abilities.

— ■ —

Educational space is flexible so students can be found in a variety of locations doing a variety of activities (e.g., computer labs, in the auditorium, or moving through the building with a camcorder or digital camera gathering documentation for a project, or participating in literature circles).

bership only through their "discipline" lens. Before too many years have lapsed, it is quite common for schools to experiment with smaller teams of two or three members. The teachers become adept at team functioning and begin to recognize the benefits associated with smaller, more flexible teams. Curriculum integration, a skill that matures with time, can be more easily accomplished on smaller teams where teachers have wider responsibility for multiple academic outcomes. Some schools begin with smaller teams in the entry grade level and steadily increase the size of teams toward the exit grade level. As part of a yearly review, many schools assess their team structures and team assignments and make adaptations for the following year.

Staff teaching assignments on the team need not be rigidly prescribed. A team of teachers can review the curriculum they are accountable for in a given year and then determine who on the team will teach what subjects. Teams, particularly in two-grade level buildings, often will decide to remain with their students for their entire seventh and eighth grade years to optimize student advancement and capitalize on long-term teacher-student relationships.

In addition, other staff members need to be regularly available to teams. Support staff such as special education teachers or gifted instructors are often assigned to work with teams in a collaborative fashion. These staff members, in consultation with the team, decide if a set of students will be pulled out for instruction or whether the supportive education teacher will co-teach with a regular education teacher in a "push-in" setting. There are schools that include a unified arts or exploratory teacher on the teams either for a quarter, semester, or year (see Smith, Pitkin, & Rettig, 1998).

Who is assigned to a team, the number of teachers, and the relationship of the specialty staff are all done in collaboration with the building leadership team. Once school staffs decide to implement a team structure and provide adequate time and resources for teams to function, they need to provide "up-front" time prior to implementation for initial team development. This often occurs in the context of inservice days during the semester or summer prior to implementation. The teams are facilitated through a series of stages revolving around the nuts and bolts of team operation and functioning. Team goals are set, team roles and responsibilities are identified and assigned, team operating procedures are established, and team process needs are addressed. All of these items are agreed upon by all team members with the caveat that periodic adjustments may be necessary as the team begins to work. To get this kind of technical assistance, schools may hire consultants, send staff members to conferences or institutes, engage in school visitations, provide abundant books and examples gathered from other schools, or join forces through a reform network. Each avenue pursued for operating in the flexible organizational structure better prepares the teachers for this new way of working.

The school also prepares its community and students for this improved method of operation. Clear and concise messages about the benefits of this structure, examples of successful implementation, and improvements for students are all instrumental in the adoption of the flexible structure. Parents are assured that their students will be better served through this structure. Along with that assurance, parents need visible evidence of the team in action through things such as team newsletters, open houses for the team in the evening or for breakfast, team sections in the building demonstrating team and student identity, team rules and expectations, team recognitions, and team phone calls to parents in the first week of school. Since this flexible organizational structure creates a known community of learners, parents and students quickly become identified with the team, thereby increasing the response capacity of the team to pinpoint student learning needs.

Flexible Use of Time to Enhance Instruction

In flexible organizational structures, teachers begin to see possibilities for further actions. Instructional time is directly under the purview of the team. Teams have common students at common times which often means that schedules are anything but common or ordinary. Teams have large blocks of time when their students are with the teachers on the team. This block of time enables teachers on the team to adjust and rearrange the instructional time as it sees necessary in order to achieve its goals. (Hackmann & Valentine, 1998; Noland, 1998; Seed, 1998; Smith, Pitkin, & Rettig, 1998; Ulrich & Yeamen, 1999). The most flexible of teams adjusts the schedule on a week-by-week, or even at times day-by-day, basis depending on needs identified during its common planning time in keeping with the curricular goals. Academic priorities take precedent over regular periods and bells. This is not to say there is chaos in this flexible arrangement. On the contrary, teachers on the teaching team within the small learning community are attentive to where each student is at a given time and the reason for a student's placement. Since the team has a designated section of the building and the teachers meet regularly to discuss issues

—■—

Teachers utilizing the large academic block to integrate subject areas. Specially constructed or single gender instructional groups for a special math unit can be seen as well.

—■—

Administrators working closely with staff by keeping up with classroom activities through frequent formal and informal visitations.

and make adjustments, the students are actually held to a higher level of accountability than in more rigid school structures with fixed periods, bells, and extended passing periods in which students are spread across classrooms in every area of the building.

Teams maximize instructional opportunities and locations through this adaptable use of time. The team flexes its schedule to more efficiently use time whether it is for the administration of a team-wide social studies test or for the fact-finding trip to the prairie preserve. Students are immersed in problem-based experiences where important skills and competencies are addressed through real-world situations and applications.

Another outcome of the flexible organizational structure is the method in which students are organized and assigned to classes. The teachers are able to group and regroup students across the team according to students' learning needs. Students are not "locked into" the same class for an entire year. In fact, on many teams, teachers have the latitude to organize and adjust their classes as they deem appropriate. They can make changes within their classes when academic or behavioral considerations warrant. Further during an integrated instructional unit, temporary study groups can be set up for a week's worth of in-depth inquiry for the "gifted" students on the team in order to provide enrichment.

Even within the individual teacher's classroom, flexible grouping is the norm rather than the exception. Teachers differentiate instruction through the application of strategies such as collaborative learning, elaborated helping arrangements, progress-based grading, challenge activities, graphic and learning organizers. The classroom teacher identifies individual learning strengths, needs, and styles then modifies instruction accordingly. Differentiating teaching for a broad range of abilities appears to occur more often as team functioning becomes more proficient. In schools that implement flexible organizational structures well, teachers and students indicate that they are engaged more often in classroom instructional strategies that are interactive, hands-on, and challenging (Felner et al., 1997). In schools void of flexible team structures or ones which are under-resourced in terms of time for planning, classroom practices are less likely to be altered, and teachers find it more difficult to implement strategies for heterogeneous classes.

Adequate team "work" time not only magnifies a team's operating potential, but also contributes to adoption of desirable teaching strategies. The common planning time within the school day serves as a vehicle for ongoing professional

—■—

Flexibility in organization is seen in partnerships with social service agencies that allow students access to needed services (e.g., free glasses, social workers).

Observations provided by Jose C. Barillas, Thurgood Marshall Middle School, Chicago, Illinois.

development through team dialogue and problem solving, which are a natural part of team life. Within the common planning time, teachers share effective teaching strategies and support one another as they learn to expand their teaching repertoires. The learning culture established within teams shifts the outcomes for changes in curriculum, instruction, and assessment into high gear.

The Structure's the Thing

A flexible organizational structure is the framework that gives life to a developmentally responsive middle level school. The existence of such a structure utilizing teams is not the end-all and be-all, but structural changes do increase the chances that instructional changes will occur (Jenkins & Jenkins, 1998). The flexible use of time, organization, staff, space, and instructional grouping set up the relationships whereby students learn and teachers teach in a more responsive, effective manner. Through the skillful guidance of committed teams of teachers acting in the best interests of their students, their students have the chance for a lifetime of possibilities. ■

References

Alexander, W. M., & George, P. S. (1981). *The exemplary middle school.* New York: Holt, Rinehart and Winston.

Arhar, J. M., Johnston, J. H., & Markle, G. C. (1988). The effects of teaming and other collaborative arrangements. *Middle School Journal, 19* (4), 22-25.

Arhar, J. M., Johnston, J. H., & Markle, G. C. (1989). The effects of teaming on students. *Middle School Journal, 20* (3), 24-27.

Carnegie Council on Adolescent Development. (1989). *Turning points: Preparing American youth for the 21st century.* New York: The Carnegie Corporation.

Erb, T. O., & Doda, N. M. (1989). *Team Organization: Promise—practices and possibilities.* Washington, DC: National Education Association.

Erb, T. O., & Stevenson, C. (1999). What difference does teaming make? *Middle School Journal, 30* (3), 47-50.

Felner, R. D., Jackson, A. W., Kasak, D., Mulhall, P, Brand, S., & Flowers, N. (1997). The impact of school reform for the middle years: A longitudinal study of a network engaged in *Turning Points*-based comprehensive school transformation. *Phi Delta Kappan, 78,* 528-532, 541-550.

Flowers, N., Mertens, S. B., & Mulhall, P. F. (1999). The impact of teaming: Five research-based outcomes. *Middle School Journal, 31* (2), 57-60.

Flowers, N., Mertens, S. B., & Mulhall, P. F. (2000). What makes interdisciplinary teams effective? *Middle School Journal, 31* (4), 53-56.

George, P. S., & Alexander, W. M. (1993). *The exemplary middle school* (2nd ed.). Fort Worth, TX: Harcourt Brace Jovanovich.

George, P. S., & Oldaker, L. (1985). *Evidence for the middle school.* Columbus, OH: National Middle School Association.

Gruhn, W., & Douglass, H. (1947). *The modern junior high.* New York: Ronald Press.

Hackmann, D. G., & Valentine, J. W. (1998). Designing an effective middle level schedule. *Middle School Journal, 29* (5), 3-13.

Jenkins, K. D., & Jenkins, D. M. (1998). The Brown Barge experience: Integrating curriculum in a total quality school. *Middle School Journal, 29* (4), 14-27.

Johnston, J. H., Markle, G. C., & Arhar, J. M. (1988). Cooperation, collaboration, and the professional development of teachers. *Middle School Journal, 19* (3), 28-32.

Noland, F. (1998). Ability grouping plus heterogeneous grouping: Win-win schedules. *Middle School Journal, 29* (5), 14-19.

Seed, A. (1998). Free at last: Making the most of the flexible block schedule. *Middle School Journal, 29* (5), 3-13.

Smith, D. G., Pitkin, N. A., Rettig, M. D. (1998). Flexing the middle school block schedule by adding non-traditional core subjects and teachers to the interdisciplinary team. *Middle School Journal, 29* (5), 22-27.

Ullrich, W. J., & Yeamen, J. T. (1999). Using the modified block schedule to create a positive learning environment. *Middle School Journal, 31* (1), 14-20.

Original article appeared in the May 1998 issue of *Middle School Journal, 29* (5), 56-59.

12. Programs and Policies that Foster Health, Wellness, and Safety

Jean Schultz

T*his We Believe: Developmentally Responsive Middle Schools* describes the essential elements from which the foundation for successful schooling of young adolescents is constructed. *This We Believe* underscores the importance of health programming for young adolescents when it states that in a developmentally responsive middle school "an emphasis on health, wellness, and safety permeates the entire school" (National Middle School Association, 1995, p. 30). How well has this essential element been actualized in your middle school?

- Can you map attention to student health across the curriculum, describe student outcomes, or demonstrate the assessment of health-related skills, concepts, attitudes, and behaviors?
- Are you able to identify those ports of safety within the school building where students may seek shelter from, and assistance with, the frequently rough waters of adolescence?
- Can you demonstrate the connectedness of school and community services, instructional components, and planned reinforcement that create a coordinated, caring community of learners?

Acknowledging that health-promoting schools are essential to the academic and personal success of young adolescents assigns fundamental status to the placement of health in exploratory, related arts, or family/consumer/life skills education. Responsive middle schools promote health not only among students but among all faculty in a wide range of school experiences. The support of health-related skills and concepts by all school personnel is consequently no longer relegated to accidental reinforcement, concomitant learning, or the teachable moment.

> Developmentally responsive middle level schools provide abundant opportunities for students to achieve and maintain healthy minds and bodies and to understand their own growth.

A review of past practice reveals only cursory attention to health programming as an essential element in middle level schools. Therefore, in order for "health, wellness and safety to permeate the entire school," all educators must accept and personalize the inclusion of a health focus in their work at the middle level. All educators have a part to play in promoting healthful behaviors while reducing risky behaviors among young adolescents. This is an expectation rarely mentioned in professional preparation programs or even at school sites. In an effort to "promote the growth of young adolescents as ... increasingly competent, self-sufficient young people who are optimistic about their future" (National Middle School Association, 1995, p. 10) teachers must focus their health promotion efforts.

There are three major reasons for educators to embrace this fundamental challenge.

Reasons to Promote Wellness

1. Poor health practices drain resources from education.

In the broadest sense, teachers and educational administrators must be alert to the financial impact poor health practices have on dollars earmarked for education in this country. Consider and ponder these points.

Medical care costs continue to rise:
- If current trends continue, less than 50% of children will be covered by employment-related health insurance in the year 2000. This represents expensive emergency room and other clinic costs borne by all citizens. (Children's Defense Fund, 1995, p. 29)
- Poor families lack the funds necessary for office visits to primary care physicians. Illnesses that could effectively be treated early are not treated until they become acute. Office visits are replaced with costly emergency room care.

Chosen behaviors impact personal health and subsequent costs:
- The elimination of tobacco use alone, either through the prevention of its initial use or through cessation of its current use, could prevent over 400,000 deaths annually from cancer, heart and lung diseases, and stroke. (U. S. Department of Health and Human Services, 1995, p. 4)

When *programs and policies that foster health, wellness, and safety are in place, an observer might see, hear, or feel...*

— ■ —

Active leadership at both district and building levels recognize and reinforce the relationship between health status and academic achievement.

— ■ —

The School Health Advisory Council that includes partners from the medical, business, criminal justice, legislative, faith, and higher education communities is scheduled to meet this week according to a notice in the daily bulletin.

- The prevention of underage drinking and excess alcohol consumption could prevent nearly 1,000,000 deaths annually, particularly by reducing deaths from motor vehicle crashes, falls, drownings, and other alcohol related deaths. (U. S. Department of Health and Human Services, 1995, p. 4)
- Better dietary and exercise patterns can contribute significantly to reducing conditions like heart disease, stroke, diabetes, and cancer, and could prevent 300,000 deaths annually. (U. S. Department of Health and Human Services, 1995, p. 4)
- The financial burden of heart disease and stroke amounts to about $135 billion a year. The annual health care and related costs attributable to alcohol abuse are $98.6 billion. The yearly costs of tobacco use amount to about $65 billion a year. (U. S. Department of Health and Human Services, 1995, p. 4)

— ■ —

The school-specific plan developed by the School Health Advisory Council establishes priorities based on a shared understanding of community values and student, family, and staff needs.

Shortfalls in health care dollars place education appropriations at risk. Because public education is contingent upon public funds, educators are wise to advocate for systemic community and school district action around student health issues. This effort is particularly critical at the middle level where young adolescents are most receptive to positive health messages and prevention strategies. With systemic support, educators can work to modify risky behaviors and reinforce positive health practices among our youth, thereby increasing our society's quality of life and positively influencing the pool of public funds available for education.

2. Students in poor health do not learn as well.

As educators, our primary job cannot be done unless we somehow address competing needs that students bring through the schoolhouse door each day. Students who need dental care, are undernourished, are under-nurtured, affected by substance abuse, or do not feel safe cannot focus their attention on learning. Educators must work together to enable students to come to school "ready to learn." (National Education Goals Panel, 1995, p. 10)

As educators we understand that

- Students who are emotionally, physically, and socially healthy are better learners and will be primed to compete for good jobs in a global labor market.

101

• High academic achievement cannot be attained or sustained if students' competing health needs go unaddressed.

Heightened academic achievement for all can be realized only when educators and the community invest in school-wide strategies to reduce behaviors that compromise student success. Our national economy and societal health depend, in part, upon accomplishing this task.

3. Youthful choices affect health.

In the past, health was largely compromised by an array of diseases (rubella, whooping cough, diphtheria, pneumonia, tuberculosis). Today, the quality and quantity of healthy life is primarily determined by *what we choose to do*. Through a national survey of adolescent behaviors called *Youth Risk Behavior Survey* (Kolbe, Kann, & Collins, 1993 p. 2), the Centers for Disease Control and Prevention has identified six behaviors which are causing premature mortality and morbidity among American youth. From survey results, it is apparent that these widespread behaviors undermine health and the resulting capacity for personal success during adolescence and adulthood. These high priority risk behaviors are

- behaviors that result in injuries both unintentional and intentional
- tobacco use
- alcohol and other drug use
- sexual behavior
- dietary behavior
- physical inactivity

Many existing prevention and management services designed to address the above problems are funded categorically. The constrictive nature of this funding stream encourages symptomatic attention (separate programming for substance abuse, suicide prevention, tobacco use) rather than holistic, collaborative attention to the interrelated and precursor problems of youth at risk.

Risk-laden behaviors are complex because they develop through the interactions of persons and circumstances within and outside the student's school experience. Therefore, it is important to enlist persons, agencies, and organizations inside and outside of the school to challenge these confounding behaviors. During this time of shrinking resources and increas-

The faculty/staff handbook sets forth a learner-centered, skill-based, comprehensive health education curriculum that is sequential and includes a minimum of forty hours of instruction per grade level.

ing need, the synthesis of new associations between existing and potential student support services is a necessity. New curricular alliances within schools are also needed. Only through holistic organizations that attend to underlying problems can schools and communities address health issues that compromise children's lives.

Each year teachers attempt to engage children whose ability to attend to instruction is diminished in some way. Unfortunately, this occurs during a time of shrinking district resources, increasing class size, and attacks on a public education system that educates more youth to a higher degree than ever before. Health programming that links school and non-school support systems and services assists teachers by providing an improved safety net for students in need, thus freeing students and teachers to focus on learning tasks. Our current loosely-coupled, differently-funded, and largely unfocused efforts miss too many children and burden teachers with too many health-related management concerns.

Can schools affect individual health as well as academic outcomes? How does a school incorporate "an emphasis on health, wellness, and safety that permeates the entire school?" The following discussion describes actions which assist in moving toward a health-enhancing middle school.

— ■ —

Displays and posters throughout the school indicate both health issues and safety are receiving attention.

Laying a Foundation for Health Promotion

Community response

Although poor student health may negatively affect academic learning, the school need not tackle student health problems alone. Indeed, most often informed community groups successfully spearhead action on behalf of young adolescents. A community-based exploration of local concerns, county or city health-related statistics, and an assessment of student needs will reveal that there are many issues a community can choose to address on behalf of children. School and community collaboration can result in healthful practices for young adolescents. Though overworked and underused, the African proverb, "It takes an entire village to raise a child" is the core of health promotion and disease prevention for young adolescents.

Many handbooks and guides are available to assist in the collaborative, task-force process. *Health Is Academic: A Guide to Coordinated School Health Programs* (Teachers College Press, 1998) is but one of the many resources educators may enlist. Only by seeking involvement and support of the community as a whole, will the "entire village" become part of the health promotion picture.

A school response

In addition to creating links to the community, a school can weave positive health practices and messages into its formal and informal curriculum (see MacLaury, 2000). A requisite to almost all other health-related initiatives is the establishment of a healthy school environment (Wisconsin Department of Public Instruction, 1997, p. 6). Although considerations such as appropriate light and ventilation as well as regular building maintenance contribute to a healthy school environment, the definition is expanded to include the implementation of policies and practices that protect and promote student's emotional, social, and mental health.

How does a school assess it's environment? A coordinated school health program assessment tool developed by the Wisconsin Department of Public Instruction assists school personnel in examining their school environment. In part, the assessment tool includes:

Culture
1. Respect between and among students, staff, and parents is reflected in the hallway, classroom, cafeteria, and bus.
2. All adult school staff are role models or mentors who foster positive and healthy behaviors.
3. School provides an environment conducive to parental involvement in the policies related to the health and safety of children.
4. Students, teachers, other school staff, administration, and parents feel safe on the school grounds, at school-sponsored events, and on school-sponsored transportation.

Physical
5. The physical environment inside and outside the school building is kept clean, safe, and well maintained.
6. The school buildings and activities are accessible to all students.
7. Schools are equipped with adequate communications systems for quick accessibility and response in emergency situations.
8. Students have a clean, cheerful, and attractive serving and dining area.

— ■ —

The professional development program plan for the year includes attention to the school-wide health plan.

9. Students and staff are given sufficient time for serving, eating, and cleaning up after meals.

Services

10. All food served or sold on campus (school cafeteria, vending machines, fund raising) supports healthy food choices.
11. Schools have in place a plan to provide health and safety training and services (e.g., first aid, CPR, crisis management, and disaster preparedness).
12. An effective working relationship exists between school personnel and community health services regarding the health and well-being of children.

Policies

13. The school's policies regarding health and safety issues are regularly discussed with school staff.
14. The school has clear policies regarding the reporting of behavior problems and legal infractions.
15. Students and parents participate in the creation of school policies regarding health and safety issues.
16. A spirit of openness, honesty, and the opportunity for expression of opinion exists among students, staff, and administration.
17. Students, parents, and school staff feel that all school policies regarding health and safety issues are implemented and enforced consistently and equitably.
18. Board policy clearly articulates and supports an intradistrict and school-to-community communication system which ensures confidentiality (Wisconsin Department of Public Instruction, 1997, p. 4-6).

Each member of the school population deserves to feel and be welcomed and safe at school. Gerald Bourgeois has provided guidance born of long experience for creating safe, inviting schools for young adolescents (Erb, 2000). School programs that foster responsibility, respect, and caretaking of emotional as well as physical health enable a school to become a welcoming and safe place for everyone.

With young adolescents, the achievement of academic success, for example, is highly dependent upon their other developmental needs being met.

—■—

The professional development program plan for the year includes attention to the school-wide health plan.

Observations provided by Bob Davis, Walsh Middle School, Framingham, Massachusetts.

An individual response

Beginning teachers are frequently amazed and appalled at the variety of student concerns that are before them each day. These concerns have little to do with academic content and everything to do with the lives of the children. Students who are in abusive relationships, involved with drugs, neglected, sexually abused, anorexic or bulimic, burdened with adult responsibility, depressed, pregnant, ill, poorly clothed, undernourished, afraid to go home, afraid to walk to school or pass in the halls, painfully shy, or sexually harassed cannot attend fully to academic achievement. Veteran teachers, no longer amazed, work to connect students with resources or provide a supportive environment. What else can an individual teacher do? Actually, quite a lot.

First, inquire regarding the status of the movement toward a comprehensive school health program in one's school or school district. Persons located within the State Department of Education or State Department of Health are familiar with the comprehensive/coordinated school health program model (Kolbe & Allensworth 1987). In addition, various national organizations representing school boards, teachers, principals, superintendents, and other professionals are working to assist their members in this arena. Raising the issue and expressing an interest may get this ball rolling in one's school or school district.

Second, inquire regarding the health-related skills which are taught in a variety of prevention programs. In collaboration with the entire staff, choose one for school-wide emphasis. For example, many alcohol and drug prevention programs include a decision-making component. Do all faculty members know this component? Is each language arts teacher well-grounded enough to use the model while discussing a short-story character? How might this component be used by a social studies teacher in discussing a recent event? Does the health educator transfer this component to food choices? Does the physical educator use this component to assist students in problem-solving?

Skill development is *not* skill inoculation. Negotiation, coping, decision-making, and refusal skills must be revisited, reinforced, reinterpreted through experience in order to be useful in the lives of young adolescents. All teachers, if they are familiar with a skill, can use their own academic content to teach and reinforce this skill.

Third, educators can help community people to see what educators see, and know what educators know regarding the health-related problems that negatively affect academic achievement. Educators can advocate for others to bring student health-related problems to the school-community table.

Conclusion

For the students that are before us each day, there is no better time than now to develop a school that is safe, welcoming, and emphasizes wellness and health. Fashioning a middle level school in which "an emphasis on health, wellness, and safety permeates the entire school" is no less important than the other characteristics of a developmentally responsive middle level school. The development of a coordinated school health program will provide an organizing framework for dealing with student health needs. Although there is much to do, there are also sources of information and guidance. Seek assistance, ask questions, and begin the process on behalf of young adolescents. ■

References

Children's Defense Fund. (1995). *The state of America's children yearbook*. Washington, DC: Author.

Erb. T. O. (2000). Interview with Gerald Bourgeois: Voice of experience on school safety. *Middle School Journal, 31* (5) 5-11.

Kolbe, L., & Allensworth, D. (1987). The comprehensive school health program: Exploring an expanded concept. *Journal of School Health, 57* (10), 409-412.

Kolbe, L., Kann, L., & Collins, J. (1993). Overview of the Youth Risk Behavior Surveillance System. Public Health Reports. *Journal of the US Public Health Service, 108* (Suppl.1), 1-2.

MacLaury, S. (2000). Teaching prevention by infusing health education into the advisory program. *Middle School Journal, 31* (5) 51-56.

National Education Goals Panel. (1995). *Building a nation of learners*. Washington, DC: U. S. Government Printing Office.

National Middle School Association. (1995). *This we believe: Developmentally responsive middle level schools*. Columbus, OH: Author.

Wisconsin Department of Public Instruction. (1997). *Component quality: A comprehensive school health program assessment tool*. Madison, WI: Author.

U. S. Department of Health and Human Services. (1995). *Healthy people: 2000 midcourse review and 1995 revisions*. Washington, DC: Public Health Service.

Original article appeared in the September 1998 issue of *Middle School Journal, 30* (1), 53-56.

13. Comprehensive Guidance and Support Services

Sherrel Bergmann

Providing successful guidance and support services for middle level students is a challenge that has been around since educators began recognizing and assessing social and emotional characteristics that affect students' academic performance. Early middle school writings made strong statements about the role of the school in meeting the emotional needs of young adolescents.

In 1902, when the period of adolescence was first being discussed in relationship to schooling, Brown (1902) in *The Making of Our Middle Schools*, stated that

> This is a period of functional acquisition and re-adjustment. Mental change and physical activity appear in intellectual awakening, the storm and stress of doubt, the conversions, the intense emotional life, the fluctuating interests and enthusiasms, the general instability, and not infrequently the moral aberrations and perversities. (p. 411)

This early writing also encouraged teachers to understand this age group and their emotional and social needs, and serve as proper moral examples of positive adulthood.

As the middle school concept gained momentum, nearly every early piece of writing that described the ideal school for young adolescents identified guidance as a viable and essential part of the middle level program. What seemed to be the cornerstone of the guidance component was that every student should have an adult in the building who was his or her advocate, and, if possible, experiences that are related to the issues of growing up (Alexander, 1969; Eichhorn, 1966; Noar, 1961; Van Til, Vars, & Lounsbury, 1967).

After almost one hundred years of documented need for advocacy and guidance in the middle level school we must ask the question heard by all parents on long trips: "Are we

> Young adolescents live in an environment that presents them with many choices. Students bring events in their out-of-school lives to school. Developmentally responsive middle level schools, therefore, provide both teachers and specialized professionals who are readily available to offer the assistance many students need.

there yet?" The answer is "no." Some schools are closer than others, but too many still relegate their guidance responsibilities to one counselor or social worker and a brief administrative homeroom and then hope for the best. An extended, proactive guidance model must be evident in every building if our students are to survive their own culture, society's early demands on them, and the school as a social system.

If we are to make progress in the area of advocacy and guidance services, then middle level schools must systematically answer several questions. Answering these questions will allow schools to design and implement guidance and support services that are appropriate to the students of their communities. A guidance task force should be convened to explore what currently exists in the school, what is needed by the students, and what is possible given the community in which the school is located. Even those schools that have what they consider to be adequate guidance services should evaluate their services annually to determine if the needs of the current students are being met.

Question #1: Who are our students and what do we know about them?

The staff of a midwestern middle school recently decided to explore the affective component of its curriculum to determine whether or not there was a need for a formalized advocacy program. Many faculty comments had been made about the changing needs of the students and the "baggage" being brought to school that was having an impact on student achievement and attitude. Current students appeared to be less respectful, less responsible, and less eager to be involved in school events. Fewer students than ever were involved in after-school activities. While the school had an excellent academic record and a seven-minute homeroom every day, the teachers felt that something was missing. While researching the demographic data of their school community the task force discovered that there were many extremes. One seventh grade homeroom teacher reported that of his twenty students

- one lived in a house with an indoor pool and bowling alley, while one came from the local homeless shelter
- nine lived with single parents, nine lived with both parents who worked, and two lived with grandparents
- four had never been out of their county, while three had been to Europe; two were born in China
- six had older siblings in the school, while three were only children

When comprehensive guidance and support services are in place, an observer might see, hear, or feel...

— ■ —

When asked, every student can name the adult that is his or her assigned advocate.

— ■ —

Counselors are present in the school and spend the majority of their time with students.

- seven distinct cultures were represented
- four were identified as gifted, and seven were receiving help for learning disabilities
- fifteen had a best friend, five did not
- seventeen had been at this school the year before; three had not
- six walked to school; fourteen rode the bus
- ten were involved in after-school activities; ten were not
- the range in height was 4'6" to 6'

All of this information had been relatively easy to determine by reading enrollment data, by observation, or simply by asking students. Given the variances in this information, the task force wondered what other differences and similarities students brought to that one group.

A general discussion with the seventh grade counselor helped the task force to understand that there were many serious problems that seventh graders brought to school with them. The counselor, with the help of county social services, was dealing with students of abusive parents, students of alcoholic parents, students who were wards of the court, students who were being shuffled between parents, students who had physical illnesses, and ones who had been in trouble with the law. While the caseload for the counselor was increasing, the time to assist students with the normal day-to-day school functions was decreasing. The counselor had no time to offer the problem-solving mini-course that had been offered in the past. Contacts with parents of students who were having academic difficulties were becoming less frequent.

More students were falling through the cracks. While teams in the school discussed students who were having problems, no one was creating a net for those students who continued to slip through. No one was a proactive advocate for all students, and the entire counseling program was reactive because of the special needs of an increasing number of students.

The task force needed to develop a vision of what was possible in its own school. While the school mission statement said that it was to assist in the development of respectful, responsible citizens, that development was being left to chance via an occasional lesson in a class or modeling of the teachers.

The task force identified several programs already in the curriculum that dealt with specific guidance issues. *DARE* was offered to sixth graders and *Snowflake* was available to all students who wished to participate. These anti-drug programs were successful, but there was nothing formal for eighth graders.

— ■ —

A specific, overall curriculum plan for guidance-related issues exists. This assures that all students receive accurate and continuous information in a non-threatening environment.

— ■ —

The counselors, in addition to being "on call," follow a schedule that assures their regular participation in team meetings.

Guidance issues were a part of the health curriculum, but that was only offered in a nine-week exploratory. Most teams had some type of student recognition program, but there was nothing consistent among the faculty. While teachers readily acknowledged that they noticed changes in student attitude, behavior, and achievement, they were not sure what they could do except refer troublesome students to the counselor.

When a school sets out to provide comprehensive guidance and support services, there must be input from teachers, counselors, students, parents, and community representatives from youth service agencies. There should be a task force that explores all possible options before a program is implemented. Frequently, adults design these services without student input, and then wonder why the students are not receptive. Too often, the role of the counselor or social worker is not clear to all clients, and the person in that job becomes, inappropriately, an administrative assistant.

— ■ —

In the faculty handbook there is a well-defined plan to keep any student from falling through the cracks.

Question #2: How are guidance and support services currently handled in our school? Who does what, when, and for whom?

Those involved in planning must be fully aware of what is currently occurring in the school. A middle school should keep what is working, drop what is not, and change whatever needs to be changed in order to provide guidance services for all students. A brainstorming session at a faculty meeting may lead to an impressive list of services and guidance-related lessons provided by groups and individuals within the school. It will show who is currently receiving services and who is being missed. Community agencies and the services they supply to young adolescents must also be explored and a list made available to all faculty members. The role of the counselor or social worker must be clearly articulated to all students, staff, and parents.

Question #3: What are the basic components we must have in our school to meet the guidance needs of our students?

One basic tenet of developmentally responsive middle level schools is that all adults are advocates for young adolescents. Each student should have one adult who knows and cares for that individual and who supports that student's academic and personal development. (National Middle School Association, 1995). A middle level school that is extending its guidance services must first establish an advocate for every student.

A comprehensive guidance program in a middle level school also requires that the school have counselors or social workers who possess skills in working with students, teachers, and parents. Cole (1981) listed the four roles of the middle school guidance worker as *counseling, consulting, coordinating,* and *functioning as a specialist* in certain areas of the curriculum.

One or two counselors cannot possibly be advocates for all of the students. They can, however, assist teachers in being advocates for students. The teacher as an advocate is a positive role model for all students and supports the academic and personal development of a small group of students.

Teachers who serve as advocates are valuable communication links among students, teachers, and families. In most middle schools advocates communicate with parents and represent the school or team at conferences. Advocates recognize change in the behaviors, achievement, and attitudes of their advisees and know when and how to refer students. They are an essential link between teachers and counselors. Advocates should have a regularly scheduled time of day when they meet with all of their advisees. This time, historically called homeroom, is now more frequently referred to as advisory or homebase.

Successful advisory programs have been those that have set advocacy as their primary purpose. These middle level schools have faculties with a professional purpose of advocating for students. Students, parents, and the community know why they have advocacy in the school and how it works. These programs are proactive and designed to help students navigate the day-to-day activities of middle school. For example, many schools use agendas or assignment notebooks to help students get organized. These notebooks are checked by the advocate who communicates with parents if the student is falling behind or not completing work. That advocate would ask the counselor to intervene if he/she thought the problem had a social or emotional cause. It is the advocate that the parents can call if the student is ill or absent from school. It is the advocate that can help the student communicate effectively with another teacher or adult. It is the advocate that checks in with the student daily. It is the advocate that encourages students to get involved in school activities.

Question #4: What advocacy programs are available?

Successful guidance programs are those that have clearly defined the role of the advocate and then offered teachers the

— ■ —

The school handbook defines the role of the advisers and lists the members of the school's standing guidance committee.

112

professional assistance they needed to carry out this role. Teachers have been taught to do active listening, one-on-one conferencing, conflict resolution, and small group facilitation. They have been given time in the daily schedule to meet with their advisees.

A secondary purpose of many successful guidance programs has been to offer a positive consistent peer group that is offered a curriculum consisting of topics related to study skills, problem solving, respect for self and others, community service, and goal setting. Each school must develop its own purpose and goals based on the culture of the students that attend the school in any given year. A faculty must know its students in order to develop the most age and community appropriate program possible. The time spent on various topics should vary with the community, the age group, and the advocacy group. All activities of the group should be purposeful and lead to a common goal. If the goal of the program is to help the students become better problem solvers, then opportunities for solving problems should be in the curriculum.

There are no firm "rules" for scheduling advocacy and guidance programs. Homebase, advisory time, block time, interdisciplinary team time, and guidance-based units are all ways in which schools provide opportunities for advocates to meet with their advisees. A typical weekly schedule for an advisory might include

> **Monday:** Get organized for the week: check the calendar, set goals, and take a trip to the school store. Students answer questions for this week's one-on-ones.
> **Tuesday:** One-on-ones. The advocate meets briefly with each student while others are reading, writing in their journals, or working on independent enrichment projects. During advocacy conference, a student shares with the teacher her or his goals for the week and responses to the questions written on Monday. Questions may include: *What is your easiest subject this month and why? What is the best thing that happened to you last week? What help do you need at school? What would you like to accomplish this week?*
> **Wednesday:** Advocate finishes one-on-ones with the group.
> **Thursday:** Group works on planning community service project or other activity such as study skills or problem solving.

— ■ —
The schedule includes a daily 25-minute period for advisories to meet.

Observations provided by Linda Holdorf, lead teacher, Jeffrey Middle School, Naperville, Illinois.

Friday: Group works on independent enrichment project, debriefs the week, and gets organized for the weekend. In some schools, they review the goals of the week and share results.

What middle schools should avoid doing is offering teachers a hodgepodge of activity sheets that are not connected to a specific purpose or goal. When a curriculum is written for student advocates it must be based on specific needs of the groups in that school and should not be a copy of one someone else has used. Sixth graders may be similar in different locations, but they are not the same. Sixth graders should not have the same curriculum as eighth graders.

What works in one school may be considered a waste of time or inappropriate in another. If the primary goal of the program is problem solving, then teachers must be given a variety of ways to meet that goal in their group. They must be able to use an activity or project that fits their own style. While some groups and teachers prefer written activities, others prefer discussion or hands-on projects. While one advocate shares a hobby with his or her group, another may prefer journal writing or reading a novel to the group to meet the same goal.

Counselors and social workers should be an integral part of the team that writes the curriculum for advocates. If substance abuse and other serious topics are to be a part of the guidance program, they must be done in concert with the local agencies that have a multitude of resources. Counselors can assist teachers in connecting with those agencies that provide the most recent references for students.

Question #5: Once we have answered the questions, what do we do?

Once the assessment of student needs, current offerings, and possible program adjustments has been completed, the guidance task force must put its ideas and findings into a plan of action. This plan should cover at least a three-year time frame and include what guidance services will be offered to students at each grade level. The plan should include a clear job description of the guidance personnel and a statement that defines the role of the advocate. Some schools have also clearly stated that advocacy is not psychoanalysis, heavy counseling, study hall, or a substitute for counseling.

The plan should also provide support for training teachers as advocates and for coordinating the program. The task force should present its plan to the faculty, parents, and students to see if there are other issues that have arisen since the task force began its work. When everyone is in agreement with the basic guidance plan, it should be presented to the school board for approval and funding. This process should be ongoing, and not thought of as a onetime event.

While many middle level schools have made progress in providing guidance services for students and have excellent programs, they must continually assess and revise their services to meet the ever-changing needs of young adolescents today. Middle level schools must be proactive as advocates so that students will have positive middle school experiences and be prepared for a successful, productive future. ∎

References

Alexander, W., Williams, E. L., Compton, M., & Prescott, D., (1969). *The emergent middle school* (2nd ed.). New York: Holt, Rinehart, and Winston.

Brown, E. (1902). *The making of our middle schools.* New York: Longmans, Green and Co.

Cole, C. (1981). *Guidance in the middle school: Everyone's responsibility.* Fairborn, Ohio: National Middle School Association.

Eichhorn, D. (1966). *The middle school.* New York: Center for Applied Research in Education.

National Middle School Association. (1995). *This we believe: Developmentally responsive middle level schools.* Columbus, OH; Author

Noar, G. (1961). *Junior high school: Today and tomorrow.* Englewood Cliffs, NJ: Prentice Hall

Van Til, W., Vars, G., & Lounsbury, J. H. *(1967). Modern education for the junior high school years.* (2nd. ed.). Indianapolis, IN: The Bobbs-Merrill Co.

Original article appeared in the November 1997 issue of *Middle School Journal, 29* (2), 55-58.

National Middle School Association

National Middle School Association, established in 1973, is the voice for professionals and others interested in the education and well-being of young adolescents. The association has grown rapidly and enrolls members in all 50 states, the Canadian provinces, and 42 other nations. In addition, 58 state, regional, and provincial middle school associations are official affiliates of NMSA.

NMSA is the only national association dedicated exclusively to the education, development, and growth of young adolescents. Membership is open to all. While middle level teachers and administrators make up the bulk of the membership, central office personnel, college and university faculty, state department officials, other professionals, parents, and lay citizens are members and active in supporting our single mission - improving the educational experiences of 10-15 year olds. This open and diverse membership is a particular strength of NMSA's

The association publishes *Middle School Journal*, the movement's premier professional journal; *Research in Middle Level Education Online*; *Middle Ground, the Magazine of Middle Level Education*; *Target*, the association's newsletter; *The Family Connection*, a newsletter for families; *Classroom Connections,* a practical quarterly resource; and a series of research summaries.

A leading publisher of professional books and monographs in the field of middle level education, NMSA provides resources both for understanding and advancing various aspects of the middle school concept and for assisting classroom teachers in planning for instruction. More than 70 NMSA publications are available through the resource catalog as well as selected titles published by other organizations.

The association's highly acclaimed Annual Conference has drawn many thousands of registrants each fall. NMSA also sponsors many other professional development opportunities.

For information about NMSA and its many services, contact the Association's headquarters office at 4151 Executive Parkway, Suite 300, Westerville, Ohio, 43081. Telephone: 800-528-NMSA; Fax: 618-895-4750; Internet: www.nmsa.org.